CHASING TOMORROW

A Collection of Poetry and Prose

LUW PRESS

CHASING TOMORROW
A Collection of Poetry and Prose
Copyright © 2020 LUW Press

Print ISBN: 978-0-9882367-8-3

Cover design by Lauren Makena

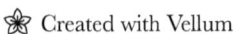 Created with Vellum

Contents

Whether we wake or we sleep,
  Whether we carol or weep,
  The Sun with his Planets in chime,
  Marketh the going of Time.

- Edward Fitzgerald

ONE

SEATS G AND H

Krystal Gerber

Row 17, aisle seat H smelled like popcorn, college boys who forgot to shower, and raw aggression. Haylie breathed the scent deep, straightened her extra-small, #16 *DeBron* jersey, and knew she was home.

At the edge of the row, Haylie hesitated, calculating. Two seats by the aisle were some of the few open in the student section on this championship game night of Duke vs. North Carolina. A shirtless, painted Jock Guy convinced Haylie to sit in the aisle and leave a seat open between them. Shirtless jocks, especially painted blue, were not her type.

Settling into the flippy plastic seat, Haylie took a picture of the huge Cameron Stadium, jumbotron flashing and music blaring, and sent it to her dad and her three brothers with the caption: *Rivalry game. I have student hot seats. Mouseketeers, Dad, eat your heart out.*

All three brothers—the Mouseketeers, as Haylie called them, mostly because they were huge—texted back within thirty seconds from their various couches, trying to one-up her with their delicious hot wings or having painted their cars blue for the rivalry game. But Haylie only grinned, knowing she had them beat. This was as good as it got for Duke fans.

Well, almost. If only her family were here. It wasn't fun, not having someone to punch when there was a bad referee call. Or being there for someone else to punch.

"Sorry, is that seat taken?"

Looking up from her phone, Haylie squinted through the glare of the stadium lights. A Duke guy was pointing at seat G, giving Haylie a half-second to study him. Carrot-colored hair that looked like it wouldn't stay combed framed an eager, chiseled face. Friendly eyes, bright as blue Gatorade, glanced over the court and then at Haylie.

"Uh, no," said Haylie, while cranking her neck to look up at him. "No one's sitting there."

"Thanks!" The stranger easily climbed over Haylie. His calves in front of her eyes were like a frog's—muscly and long.

"Phoof," said he, falling into his seat. The newcomer was almost silenced beneath the roar of the crowd as the lights dimmed and drums thundered. "Almost missed them coming out of the tunnel. Would have sucked."

Haylie understood completely. When Duke played North Carolina, diehard fans showed up for the tunnel appearance. It wasn't a rivalry game without it. Still, sitting there waiting for tip-off, she'd never been so distracted. Carrottop was shifting in his seat, eyes glued to the court—and Haylie couldn't help noticing the way one curl fell over his fine forehead.

He's hot, she thought in wonder. *A hot redhead at close proximity. Huh.*

Then it was tip-off, and Haylie forget the young man in seat G —mostly. After all, it was criminal in her family to let attraction get in the way of the game, and what a lethal game! The players were out for legal blood. The first five minutes were scoreless, red and blue fighting for ground, for a basket.

"What the foul?" Haylie exploded, as the referee delivered the ball to the enemy. Haylie had a long list of basketball-tailored epithets, since cursing was forbidden in her house and you had to express your outrage somehow.

At the first media time-out, when the roar of the packed student section had subsided to a contained bedlam, Haylie was surprised when Carrottop spoke up suddenly, "You can just do it you know."

Blinking up at him—even sitting down, she had to look up—Haylie asked warily, "Do what?"

"Smack me." Hot Carrot-top turned back to the court. "You lifted your fist like five times when we lost possession or the other team got a free-throw. Just punch me next time. My little brother does."

"Really?"

He smiled. When he smiled, Hot Carrottop became devastating. "Really. You love basketball huh?"

Haylie tried to smirk. "You're the first guy not to ask if I *liked* it."

Carrottop shrugged. "You almost punched a stranger five times in the first quarter. You're wearing a DeBron jersey, who is only the best guard *ever* at Duke. He's headed for the NBA, first draft. On top of that, you've had to stand in line for hours to get a seat, just like me. You *gotta* love it."

"You love DeBron too?" Haylie leaned in closer and found she could feel the heat coming off him.

"Yeah," said he, not leaning away.

"That deserves a name then." Haylie thrust out a hand. "Haylie."

"Ben," said Carrottop, gripping her hand and squeezing it. Haylie liked it—and was surprised.

Suddenly a little bashful, carrottop Ben unsuccessfully tried to make himself smaller, sinking low in his seat as the game started up again. Haylie found herself doing the same, wishing she had an excuse for leaning against him and feeling foolish for wishing it.

In a mere five minutes, Duke pulled ahead with four three-pointers in a row, and Haylie screamed herself nearly hoarse, jumping up and down beside Ben as the shirtless blue-painted Jock Guy jumped up and down on Ben's side, waving a stereotypical foam finger.

To celebrate, cheerleaders shot special rivalry T-shirts into the crowd. Using every inch of her five-foot-two reach, Haylie didn't come close to catching one. But Ben did.

"Here," said Ben. "I've got one at home already."

Haylie accepted the shirt with a grateful nod and a pleasant tingle down her spine. "Well, I don't have one. Behold my lifelong sorrow. I'm shorter than a push broom, and I love basketball."

"Not for the faint of heart?"

"Or of skull."

"Brothers?"

"You got it."

As the buzzers blew for half-time, Haylie, having been conscious of an odd tension building on Row 17, a tension that had nothing to do with being five points behind, was eager to get up and get away. But she was halted by a huge, gentle hand on her arm.

"Wait," said Ben. Reaching over, he unsnagged Haylie's ponytail from her seat, causing a shiver to go clear to her sneakered toes. "There. It won't hurt now."

"Huh," said Haylie, rubbing at her sudden goosebumps and trying not to stare at his blue, blue eyes.

"*Hey, hey, hey Duke fans! Are you ready for a contest?*" The emcee's voice thundered out of the speakers, and the swiftly emptying rows halted.

Haylie, competitive in all things, even corny half-time contests, perked up at once.

"*Kissssss Caaaam!*"

Freezing, Haylie refused to look right or left, grateful she was in an aisle seat.

"*But waaaiiit! Whoever wins best Kiss Cam gets to meet Duke guard, the incredible DeBron, for lunch at our sponsor's Greek-my-Freak eatery. He might even sign something, if you ask nice. Winners announced after the game! Now, make some noooise! Show me who's ready to win?!*"

At once, Ben and Haylie looked at each other, and Haylie felt herself, the tomboy, the hard-hitter, the fourth Mouseketeer, blush. It was a miracle that left her speechless. Usually, Haylie had a strict no Kiss Cam policy, let alone blush policy, even though she'd never had to enforce it. But a face-to-face meeting with star DeBron was on the line, along with this electric, endearing Ben.

"Meet DeBron?" said Ben in awe.

"You sound like a fangirl," said Haylie, recovering her powers of speech.

"No."

"You do."

"So do you."

"It's *DeBron.*"

"Still."

"Yeah," Haylie said, a little breathlessly. "Besides, Kiss Cams never fall on the student section anyway."

"You thought of this before?"

"Well, I have come to a lot of games since freshman year, and I've gone on bad dates with guys in the student section before," Haylie said defensively, trying to disguise her ramping up heartbeat.

"Lots of guys, huh?'

"Maybe two." Haylie admitted, feeling herself flushing impossibly again.

"Now who wants to meet DeBronnnnnn?"

The stadium erupted, noisemakers whirring and blasting. Haylie felt every flicker of contrary, competitive fire burning higher as the music heightened. Lose her chance to meet DeBron? To win? To show her brothers the pictures? But to win—to really sell it—she couldn't. She liked jerseys better than pink, and guys only so long as they didn't quote wrong statistics about the Lakers. She wasn't flashy or skilled at kissing. She was way outclassed.

"Dude, I've got it," exploded Ben, grinning as he whirled in his seat to look at her.

"Dude?" Haylie all but growled, feeling the sting of defeat already.

"How about a stage kiss?" Ben put forth the idea carefully, as if afraid of getting fouled.

Haylie blinked. "Stage kiss?"

"Yeah," said Ben. "I was in *Seven Brides for Seven Brothers* once in junior high, played Gideon. At the end, when all the brothers kissed, we faked it."

"How?"

Ben waved this paltry objection away. "Don't worry. It's easy.

You don't have to do a thing. And it's just in case, you know? So there's none of that awkward stuff if the Cam falls on us. Agreed?"

Haylie thought about it. She thought about her brothers, watching at home, and winced. She thought about shaking DeBron's hand. She thought about Ben's long arm, firm and warm around her waist.

"Agreed."

Already there were shrieks and hollers around the stadium as the Kiss Cam fell on couples who kissed enthusiastically, hoping to win. Haylie hardly noticed them, moths and bumblebees buzzing in her stomach as she steeled herself for the outside chance to win—and steeled herself against imagining what kissing Ben for real would be like.

As the music intensified, the shrieks grew louder, and the emcee yelled, the Kiss Cam and spotlight also flickered closer to the student section. As it did, Ben pulled a notepad out of his big pocket, quickly wrote something Haylie couldn't see, and tore the paper off.

At Haylie's curious glance he said, "We want to slam dunk this! After all, if we can't sell it for real, we ought to at least *market* it."

"Don't tell me. Marketing major."

"How'd you know?"

The spotlight flew over the crowd. The light flickered over them quickly and Haylie slumped, exchanging relieved and defeated glances with Ben.

Then, the loud, shirtless Jock Guy who Haylie had been ignoring all game stood up and waved with all his might, attracting the camera back. When the Kiss Cam saw the Jock was alone, the camera flickered over to Haylie and Ben, and the music boomed, their faces appearing pale and intense on the jumbotron.

As the hot light burned down on them and catcalls rose all over the section, Ben grinned a challenge at Haylie, who nodded gamely. Holding his "slam-dunk" paper out towards the camera in one hand, Ben put his other arm around Haylie's waist, pulling her close and dipping her over the seat. He was a gentlemen—tipping his head to block the camera's view, Ben didn't move an inch closer than agreed upon. Haylie thought she'd go insane, heart pounding, his closeness like a would-be buzzer-beater climbing all around the hoop, hovering on the edge and then falling off to the floor with a sad thump.

Haylie still hung on the precipice as the speakers boomed, catcalls shrilled through the student section, and her mouth hovered a breath away, a scarce, torturous inch away, from Ben's. In the spotlight shadow cast by Ben, they stared at each other and completely forgot basketball even existed.

The seat next to Ben jostled, Jock Guy leaping to his feet, trying to crowd in on the camera. With a jostle and a bump, Jock Guy bumped into Ben and with a gasp of surprise, Ben lost his balance, dropped his paper, and his lips fell against Haylie's with a sudden rush of heat.

Ben tried to pull away, but badly off balance, he half collapsed against the seat—then stopped fighting it. Haylie didn't blame him. She'd kissed guys before. This wasn't kissing, this was living. This was belonging and feeling and burning and home.

What the foul, thought Haylie happily, hazily, as she kissed him back, one hand reaching up to hold his wrist, finding his hand against her skin.

It had lasted four seconds, maybe five, fake and accidental kiss in all. Yet when the music changed and the spotlight shifted, Ben took half a heartbeat too long to break away, his face redder than a basketball, matching his ruddy hair. It took him another second to realize he still cradled her cheek in his hand, and he dropped it like his fingers were on fire.

"Sorry," he said, turning a shade redder, if that was possible.

"Don't be," Haylie said, meaning it.

"Dude, *awesome,*" said Jock Guy.

Ben and Haylie were strangely quiet through the fourth quarter, not even rising out of their seats for a truly genius steal in the last forty-five seconds. Ben's paper lay on the ground, neither of them daring to pick it up. They didn't touch. They pretended to be seat G and H again.

Haylie wondered if Ben too was writhing in a personal cesspool of embarrassment.

A dozen people were on that Kiss Cam, she thought. *With that awkward performance we don't have an ice cube's chance in Florida of winning, and our* accident *was just broadcasted to 25,000 people. Sneakers, I feel sick.*

The worst part, Haylie wouldn't even admit to herself. Deep in her gut she knew she wanted to kiss Ben again—this second. More than once. She also knew as all women sometimes do, whether they love jerseys more than pink or not, that Ben wanted to kiss her too. Yet she also knew, as women sometimes do, that Ben would stonily refuse to even ask for her number.

Duke was going to lose. With a nine point deficit it was obvious by the time that last steal came, too little too late. Haylie buried her face in her hands, feeling Ben leaning as far away from her as possible, like she was in an invisible penalty box.

Coward, thought Haylie, not having a clue if she meant herself or Ben.

The last time-out met uneasy, furious silence from the crowd. As the haggard players gathered around red-faced coaches on the jumbotron, Haylie had made up her mind. She wasn't going to stick around after the game to see if she—they—won. She would run, like a scared little chicken, up the cement stairs and hopefully all the way back to Connecticut.

Halfway through the time-out, as fans muttered in misery, Haylie felt Ben's gaze fall on her face. Haylie looked up into his pale face, haunted with a grimace of a smile.

"Next game, huh?"

Haylie looked and looked at him and smiled back, steeling her nerve. *I'll never see him again. Sports stink. Like roadkill and broken dreams.*

"Yo, yo, yo fans, we got something to annooooooounce!" blasted the emcee from the speakers. *"The game ain't over and neither are we. Our judges have decided to declare the Kiss Cam winners early so MAKE some NOISE!"*

Haylie jumped but Ben didn't. He stared at the floor.

"Looks like you'll have that first date you wanted! Lucky couple in row 17, whaaaat!"

Haylie blinked in disbelief and confusion and relief and even more embarrassment. She was too discombobulated to do more than stare as Ben picked up the notebook paper off the floor, his slam dunk, and held it up so Haylie could see what Ben had shown the Kiss Cam:

We don't know each other from Adam.

Should our 1st Date be meeting DeBron?

Haylie whooped and fist-pumped. "Way to go *slam dunk!*"

Ben grabbed her waist and hauled her petite bod clear off the concrete, waving the paper as the cam swept over them again. When Haylie stiffened, he set her down with a jolt.

"Sorry," said Ben breathlessly, not looking sorry at all. "You probably hate that."

Haylie threw her arm around Ben's waist, breathing in deep the new-sneaker smell she realized now was Ben. Smiling the smile her dad called her happy-mischief-grin, she said, "I could get used to it."

TWO

MALEVOLENT MARCH

Lorraine Jeffery

We know Maleficent January with her wretched cold
and Wicked Witch of the West February with her ice.
But you, my dear March, certainly break the mold
and you're the worst, by any roll of the dice.

You come out in a spring dress, just a little bit tight,
and sit barelegged, promising spring and green.
In like a lion and out—Nope, no lamb in sight.
You're a blatant liar, March, the worst I've ever seen.

You're the black mold on the roses,
you're the grub in the new green lawn,
you're the stillborn bud the frost exposes,
you're the hunter who kills the fawn.

Daffodils slammed back into frozen earth
way before they could bud.
Tulips with no chance of birth,
and pansies mashed in the mud.

Black slush crushes hope, every single sliver.
You promise and smile,
you flirt and beguile,
but baby, you just don't deliver.

THREE

CHASING TOMORROW

Josie Hulme

Her footsteps echo off the midnight alley walls. A cold breeze gusts down the narrow corridor, bringing a hint of rotting garbage and dank corners. Fear crawls up my spine and settles, cold and clammy, at the base of my skull. I pause a moment, but the tap of her feet draws me into the dark.

A musty heaviness fills the air, sinking to the bottom of my lungs with each gasp, muffling my breath, filling my ears with my heartbeat.

A single naked bulb hanging drunkenly from a rusty fixture throws a circle of light on the ground. The alley's broken pavement is like jagged teeth nipping at her ankles as she skirts the light. I see a flash of sky-high red heels and a flutter of her delicate dress before her creamy calf is swallowed again by the shadows.

I speed up. She's not getting away this time.

But when I get to the light, she's long gone. I push farther, faster, eager to finally feel her heat, her vitality under my fingers.

I see her silhouetted against the night-city dusk at the end of the alley. It steals the color from her, painting her in grays and blacks—tumbled curls, straight shoulders, slim waist, long legs.

I start to run.

She doesn't know I follow her. She's never seen me, never felt me watching, never perceived my yearning. Now she steps to the right, moving away again, intent on what's in front of her instead of what's behind.

Hurrying forward, I trip over a box and sprawl to the ground. Whatever was in the container rolls hollowly across the pavement. My cheek is pressed to the grit and grime of the alley. A cellophane wrapper crinkles under the fingers of my right hand, and I prefer not to question the warm, wet substance that coats my left hand.

I scramble to my feet and rush around the corner headlong into a chest as wide and hard as a brick wall. I bounce off and hit the pavement. Blinking from my new seat on the ground, I peer up at the hulking figure in front of me. He looks like a prison warden, which I guess is appropriate—hair buzzed high and tight, body like a tank, and eyes that see everything and show nothing. Words like *schedule* and *priority* and *order* are important to this guy.

I curse silently, but I keep my face pleasant. "Hey, Time. What's up?"

"Today." He says my name like it's a bad word. "Where are you headed in such a hurry?"

"Nowhere."

"Really." Time doesn't say it like it's a question, but his gray eyes stare at me like he's waiting for an answer. I keep quiet. I'm no dummy. Finally, he says, "Guess who I saw pass by here a minute ago?"

I stand and dust off the seat of my jeans. "Who?" I give him what I hope is a casually curious look.

"You can drop the innocent act," he says. His hands are fists at his side, and he's the kind of guy who would use them. "I've told you before not to chase after her."

"But—"

"But nothing. You'll never catch up to Tomorrow."

"Please, Time," I say. "She's so beautiful and mysterious."

"It's hopeless, Today."

"No, it's not." I shove my hands through my hair. "If she'd just look behind her—if she could only see me—I know she'd feel the same way I do."

"You're too different," Time says. "I know you both. Tomorrow's full of optimistic hope for the future. You're the painful, inescapable present. It won't work."

"I can change," I say, "if she'll just give me a chance."

I try to walk past him, but he plants a hand on my chest.

I turn my head, not casual any more, and give him my own unbending stare. "I have to try." His mouth is granite and his eyes are steel, but he drops his hand.

I run down the sidewalk, sprinting past barred windows impatient to dazzle passers-by, weaving through empty tables forlorn without their twenty-somethings sipping flavored coffees. I pass street lights shining for an audience of one. Me.

But no, there are two of us here. I see Tomorrow ahead, flitting through the puddles of light, feet barely touching the ground.

And I follow, like I always have.

Farther and farther she leads me. Hours and miles through the night. The city falls behind, the suburbs, the scattered houses that fringe civilization. Fields of wheat roll by, corn and grass, soybeans and rice. Oceans and mountains and deserts and wide open spaces that only small, furtive creatures call home.

Finally, light breaks in the east. I see her pause, eyes forward. The first rays of sunlight finger her golden hair, turning it into a tumble of fiery curls.

Now! I think. Now, while she stands on the threshold.

I double my speed. Close. Closer. I reach out as the sun bursts over the horizon. But I'm too late. My fingers brush the red-gold tips of her hair as she skips ahead once more.

My toe catches on the uneven ground, and I stumble. Spin around.

My heart leaps in surprise. What's this? Someone behind me with her hand outstretched, reaching for me. I meet Yesterday's eyes —pleading, wishful eyes—for one brief moment. Then I gain my balance, shake it off, and turn again to chase Tomorrow.

FOUR

THE WARNING SIGNS: ORIGINS OF AN OBSESSIVE FISHERMAN

John Saporito

Something must be wrong. Very wrong. Yes, fishing is a fun thing to do. But that's not why I fish. I fish because I have to. Clearly, there is something more than enjoyment going on here. But how did I let it get this far? How did I get here? I know that, for me, there is an inexplicable attraction to fish and to the aqueous world in which they live—and I struggle to articulate it any better than that. Perhaps this attraction is embedded somewhere in my genetic code (I do have some family members who suffer from similar afflictions, albeit in lesser degrees of severity). My fascination with fish and with the way they work has matured over time; as a man, I have either come into my own and found my way or totally lost it and gone off the deep end entirely, depending on your perspective.

No matter how you regard me these days, I do believe that fishing was destined from the very beginning to take on a prominent role in my life. Although I was not mindful of them as they transpired, my early life teemed with harbingers that support this assertion. The behaviors of my youth, whether calculated or spontaneous, were conspicuous precursors to my eventual path. In hindsight, I probably should've paid closer attention.

———

Symptoms of my—um, condition—were quick to reveal themselves. The first whiff of testimony, at least the first that I'm aware of, arose at such a juvenile age that my own memory of the event is nonexistent. It is only through the memories of those present at the time that I have any knowledge of the occasion. Considering my obvious handicap in recalling the affair, it only seems reasonable to recount it as if I were not there at all:

At the top of the indoor staircase in his family's home in suburban New York, a three-year-old boy stood chattering aimlessly in an incomprehensible toddler dialect. His mother, father, and six-year-old brother anxiously watched as the child took his first step toward their position at the bottom of the stairs. In an instant of youthful clumsiness, the boy stumbled in his descent and began to plunge, end over end, down the entire length of the staircase. Bumping and bashing his tiny frame along the way—and all the while muttering incoherently—he ultimately came to a halt with an unnerving thud at the feet of the horrified onlookers. Incredibly, he exhibited no signs of the fall; there were no tears or whimpers whatsoever to reference the mishap. Instead, vaulting to his feet, he coolly asked his bewildered family for—of all things—a fishing pole.

Now, if my fanaticism for fishing was truly preordained—or if hitting my soft, developing skull on thirteen steps had something to do with it—I'll never know. This much, however, was evident right away: there was to be a persistent, burgeoning theme in my life from that day forward.

———

Halloween costumes, those once-a-year beacons of a child's interests, are among the most visible and telling forms of youthful self-expression. There were some years when I reached for a traditional, ghoulish outfit. Other years, my Halloween attire was a direct reflection of my budding fixation. I dressed as a scuba diver one autumn, a clever homemade getup that was brought together by way of a fabricated "oxygen tank" consisting of a two-liter soda bottle wrapped in aluminum foil. And though it was tedious parading around the neighborhood in flippers, the costume itself was a commendable feat. It should come as no surprise that on multiple occasions, when the calendar settled on October's last day, I walked the streets clad as a fisherman. Also not surprisingly, I never once saw another kid dressed the same way. They tended to go for more popular selections.

This sort of thing—these departures from the norm—were rather common for me, quirks that became automatically associated with my name for anyone who knew me well during my youth.

———

These days, I fish alone. My earliest experiences with fishing were quite different, however, and always included the watchful support of older family members. My dad, in a remarkable exposition of patience, used to periodically take all five of his sons to the nearby harbor or reservoir so that we could sling baited hooks at whatever small quarry swam by. During summer vacations or time off from school, my grandpa would collect me and a brother or two to fish from one of the many docks that adorned the bays of southern New Jersey. Training us on the finer points of threading a worm onto a hook—and on how to *not* reel in our lines every thirty seconds—his outings have chiseled a permanent residence in my fishing memory. Every so often I would spend time with a few of my uncles on Long Island's ocean beaches, excursions that constituted my formal introduction to the mesmerizing domain of fishing after nightfall.

The guardians who chaperoned these initial fishing ventures were successful in provoking my fondness for the world below our own. But sporadic trips to the water were soon not enough to satisfy my desire to catch fish. It wasn't until I got my first summer job as a caddie at age thirteen that my fishing evolution truly began. For me, with added responsibility came great freedom. Each July and August afternoon, after fulfilling my obligations on the golf course, I would ride my bike to one of the local ponds or streams to soak bait for a few hours before dinner. With the company of a friend or two, many summer days were spent streamside in pursuit of the finned critters that made their homes in the area. Sometimes I fished alone and was content to do so. Enthralled by the mystery, by the understanding that anything could happen when I put a bait in the water, I relished the many youthful hours that were passed on the banks of my favorite waterways. When Labor Day came and school overtook my employment, I bemoaned the lack of fishing that would occur while the year ran its course.

I never really believed that school was where the important facets of my education took place. I simply wasn't a classroom learner. What I considered to be the more meaningful teachings of my adolescence presented themselves outdoors, far away from the blackboards and bookwork. Still, whenever a school assignment provided me the opportunity to choose a subject at my own discretion, the theme seldom varied. Whether art projects, library time, or creative writing, I regularly centered my efforts on fish-related material. The lone exception may have been a somewhat-parallel childhood infatuation with reptiles and amphibians. Teachers must have grown weary of grading my homogeneous work—provided that their sanity had not already been broken by my relentless class clowning.

I was not a bad child in school. I just never sat still, raised my hand when I had something to say, or paid attention for any significant length of time (I mean, why the hell *would* I have paid attention when I could draw pictures, make paper airplanes, or stare out the window instead?). My teachers were unable to get me to stop fidgeting in my seat, and it was usually only a young and exceptionally energetic instructor who could handle my presence. If, however, the lesson plan was tailored to hold my interest, I miraculously transformed into the teacher's pet. But these instances were rare, and I was generally left with no other option but to entertain myself in less constructive ways.

If ever there were a surplus in the federal education budget, I could envision some of my former grade school teachers lobbying to use the excess funds to erect monuments in my honor in detention halls nationwide. My ceaseless, unscripted, classroom-distracting commentary was well known by peers and faculty—each party receiving the antics in opposite fashion. During my campaign through the public education system, it was widely speculated that my behavior was the impetus that forced a few hapless teachers into early retirement. Cleaning out their desks for the final time after successfully dragging me through their curriculum, the poor souls opted to relinquish their tenure rather than risk a repeat with one of my younger siblings looming inescapably in the queue. My disruptions, which reached a notable peak when I was in middle school, became so brazen that I was given an unlimited "hall pass" that allowed me to just get up and leave class whenever I felt that an outburst was imminent. To the best of my knowledge, I am the only student in the history of American learning institutions to ever be awarded such a dubious accolade.

———

My most infamous and most often recalled episode of class clowning occurred outside the jurisdiction of the state-commissioned teachers who were entrusted with the unenviable task of regulating my conduct. On a Wednesday evening, just like any other during my youth, I was seated at an ordinary student desk for an hour of Religious Education (I had, earlier in the year, been switched into this particular class after a previous instructor gave up on me). In similar desks organized in a grid throughout the room, a band of my seventh-grade cronies were seated, eagerly anticipating the improvised stunt that they had come to expect, without fail, each class session.

Acting entirely on impulse, I decided that mid-lecture was an appropriate time to sharpen my pencil. I eyeballed the old-fashioned, crank-handle sharpener that was fastened to the windowsill across the room. My pencil, it should be known, was probably already sharper than any hook I've ever fished with. And besides, it's not as if I was actually taking notes. I rose from my seat and strode confidently toward the contraption, noting the feverish grins of my classmates as I passed. Slowly but with much enthusiasm, I began to sharpen the implement, my luckless teacher forced to elevate her voice above the racket.

Maybe it was our location in a church basement, but, whatever the origin, I was blessed with a moment of comic ingenuity. Suddenly, I cranked down on the pencil sharpener as fast as my arm would allow and—leaning back under the strain of an imaginary fish—turned to the class and shouted, "I'm reeling in a big one!"

The door slammed shut behind me; the classroom filled with laughter, which then spilled out into the hallway and followed me as I ambled its lengths, slated for a rendezvous with the principal.

Seated by the threshold of the administrative office, the mother of one of my friends was fulfilling her duties as the night's volunteer hall monitor. "What did you do this time?" she queried. I informed her, in explicit detail, of my transgression. Clearly amused, she cupped a hand over her mouth to conceal an ear-to-ear grin. With the other hand, she motioned for me to enter the chamber and complete my sentence.

———

One afternoon, sometime during the height of my classroom shenanigans, a routine fishing trip ended in the single oddest emergency room visit that I have ever been affiliated with. I was fishing with a friend in a local stream in an area we dubbed "Catfish Cove" for its abundance of brown bullhead catfish. Harboring easy catches of six-to-ten-inch bullheads, the spot offered enough continuous action to hold the concentration of a pair of young, easily distracted fishermen. We had been fishing for a few hours, hooking one cat after another on earthworms, and subsequently freeing and watching them swim off before repeating the process. The fishing was so effortless that neither one of us could have been prepared for what happened next.

As my friend brought yet another bullhead toward the stony bank, I edged closer to the water to grasp the fish for a smooth release. Abruptly—and with an utter lack of reasoning behind it—

my cohort flipped the tip of his rod, sending the fish racing skyward in a steep arc.

We watched in apprehension as the catfish, now several feet overhead, was overcome by the interminable law of gravity and began hurtling back toward earth to complete its orbit. The creature, likely the first of its species to experience aeronautical flight, elected to use my right arm as a makeshift runway—but not before extending its primitive landing gear.

I looked at my friend. I looked at the fish. For what was surely only a few seconds—but what I perceived as much, much, longer—nothing happened. The fish, still hooked, lay motionless on my arm. I waited for it to slide off, leaving a trail of slime in its wake. But it never did.

It defied logic. All reason was obliterated. In a moment of ludicrous revelation, I came to understand that the fish had somehow adhered itself to my arm. Then, as fish out of water are known to do, the eight-inch bullhead commenced to flail about in distress, which seemed to me more like animosity. Its pectoral fin, culminating in a multi-barbed spine, had embedded itself in my forearm. I dropped to my knees in pain, watching helplessly as the fish's thrashing tore through whatever tissue constituted my lanky teenage arm.

My friend, presented with an opportunity to help his wounded comrade, proceeded instead to roll on the ground in a fit of boisterous laughter.

Things soon calmed down. The fish relaxed long enough for me to take rational action. These were the days before cell phones sprouted invariably from people's hands, so my friend and I, in need of assistance, crossed the street and rang the doorbell of the nearest house. A young couple answered the door. There was a glaring need to explain the circumstances of our visit, but that need was quickly satisfied when the homeowners secured a glance of the two vexed teenagers before them, one of whom was sporting a grotesque fish-arm.

We were whisked inside and led to the kitchen, where my friend used the cordless phone to call my mom. He struggled mightily to convey the scenario to my mother, who was on her way by the time the conversation ended. One of our hosts, sensing that I was in great discomfort, called for a paramedic to come to the house.

Minutes later, all four of us were out on the porch watching an ambulance pull up to the curb. The paramedic wasted no time donning gloves for the first bid to dislodge the fish from its roost. As if it somehow anticipated the impending grapple, the bullhead started to furiously beat its tail, flooding my stricken limb with agony. The medic swiftly pinned the fish to my forearm with his radio, bringing its rampage to a halt. He then gripped the creature firmly and, with substantial force, attempted to pull it from my arm.

The fish didn't budge. No closer was the creature to removal from my arm than I was to relief from its stinging, serrated spine. The paramedic, unable to assist any further, radioed the emergency room in preparation of our arrival. My mom appeared just as the fish was being fastened to my arm with a heavy gauze wrap. After thanking the young homeowners for their help, I was ushered into the ambulance for a ride to the hospital.

My friend was left behind to atone for his angling blunder, condemned to a mile-long walk with the added burden of two bicycles, two fishing rods, and two tackle boxes.

Of the assortment of ill-fated characters who ended up in the emergency room that day, I had the distinction of being the most popular. In a show of homage to what must have seemed a phenomenal medical enigma, all the doctors and nurses lined up to catch a glimpse of the "boy with the fish stuck to his arm." One delighted nurse even snapped a few photographs to celebrate the anomaly. To impart the occasion with sufficient irony, I was led to a special examination room—one featuring wallpaper that depicted a sequence of undersea life.

And so, encircled by an array of tropical fishes, the appointed doctor got to work extracting the bullhead from my forearm. He sent a full syringe of anesthetic shooting into the site of the wound and, within minutes, was prying at the fish while a team of dumbfounded nurses gazed on.

Eventually, the bullhead was separated from my arm. But, for a short while, I was part man, part fish. One of the really amazing aspects of the event is that the catfish—hardy animals that they are —survived the ordeal. After over an hour out of water, bound tightly in dry bandaging nonetheless, the fish sprang right back to life when set in a shallow pan of hospital tap water. Baffled, I stood witness as the fish swam spirited laps around its temporary plastic habitat.

There was only one thing left to do. Following my discharge from the hospital, I was on my way back to the scene of the incident. I know there are plenty of people who would have tossed the critter into the deep fryer, but I had developed a certain measure of respect for that individual fish and its extraordinary display of resilience. As I had done so many times before with so many other catfish at that exact location, I watched contentedly as the bullhead glided away to freedom.

———

The clues were there all along. They were the road signs of my life, the emissaries of my personal destiny. There was a time when I could not hear such calls. Many people never can. But, when I did finally wake to these signals, a renaissance of sorts followed. My ambitions were forever changed, and I began to seek out my own path. To travel any other was a denial of what I truly wanted.

Not much has changed since my earliest days as a fisherman. Sure, the fish I pursue have changed in size, and the catches have changed in quantity. And, accordingly, the expectations that I set for myself have changed. Yet, when it all comes together—when I have my quarry in hand—I feel the same childlike exuberance that I felt back then, and maybe that's the clearest sign of all that I'm doing what I was born to do.

———

Here's a fun fact: I started my college career as an oceanography major. Roughly two weeks into my first semester, I withdrew from the introductory course because it was short on practical substance and therefore failed entirely to capture my focus. Afterward I transferred schools, changed majors twice, and ultimately graduated with a bachelor's degree in history. In time, I would learn about the life cycles of the sea. But, consistent with my very nature, I would do so on my own terms. Only so many of the ocean's priceless lessons can be taught within the boundaries of a classroom. And, for me, its puzzles were not to be solved there.

———

You can pick your hobbies. You can even pick your passions. But, if it runs any deeper than that—then you probably had very little say in the matter. I didn't choose fishing. Fishing chose me.

FIVE

INSOMNIATE

Robyn Buttars

Though safe and warm I ruminate
While wishing I could navigate
The path to sleep and speculate
On life while I regurgitate
Day's moments as I punctuate
The time I now contaminate
With doubts and fears I replicate.

Perhaps if I intoxicate
The drinks will help to satiate
And peace of mind disseminate
But that would only complicate
And somehow misappropriate
The thoughts I must incorporate.

I need to differentiate
The truth and how to correlate
Beliefs I must consolidate
For then my strengths can stimulate
All wisdom I would permeate.

Alone I now commiserate
Mistakes I can't articulate
My stomach churns I nauseate
And fear I'll hyperventilate
As brain cells discombobulate.

Alas, I just procrastinate
My sleep while I deliberate
And guess how others speculate
Or what they will pontificate
Though sure they will miscalculate
Will someone come and arbitrate?

For all I underestimate
But none can me incriminate
And yet I reinvestigate
The meaning they communicate—
To sleep I cannot graduate—
I swear I don't exaggerate
As in the dark I ruminate.

SIX

RUSSIAN TEA FOR TWO

Lorin Grace

"May I take this seat?"

I glance up from my book, nod at the man—yet another grad student—and return to my reading. Instead of moving the chair to another table like the two men before him, he pulls out the chair and sits down. The brown plastic lunch tray slaps against the Formica tabletop. He removes the lunch special, hot roast beef sandwich and kettle chips, and sets it on the table along with a steaming cup of tea. A scribbled line through the S marks the side. No sugar. Interesting choice.

Instinctively, I move my half-eaten sandwich closer, giving him more room, and pull my mostly empty teacup to where he won't tip it over. My focus returns to my book. The man studies me and I try to ignore him. I lift my book, forming a wall between us. The title, Война́ и миръ, puts most people off.

He clears his throat and in perfectly accented Russian asks, "*War and Peace? You read Russian?*"

I respond in my native tongue. "No, I don't. I just pretend to read 600,000-word books to keep nosy men away."

His eyes widen, as does his grin. "Your accent is Ukrainian, yes? Are you a student here? How is the linguistics master's program?"

I shut Tolstoy's masterpiece and lay it on the table face up. Conscious of the stares coming from the crowded table next to us, I answer in English. "I'm a professor. Our language programs are excellent."

"So young to be so accomplished," he whispers in Russian.

Stiffening, I gather my things. He lays a hand on my arm before I can stand. "I am sorry, I did not mean to upset you." He reverts to English. His accent is better than mine. He must not have learned English in Boston. "Please, may we talk for a few moments? I so rarely have the opportunity to converse with a fellow Ukrainian."

I do not deny my origin. I look at my watch. "Just a few minutes. I teach a class at 2:00." I'm curious. He is the only person on campus who ever noticed that I have a Ukrainian accent, including the other Russian professors. I lie to myself; the reason I'm staying has nothing to do with his eyes, the color of warm tea.

"I came to America when I was ten years old. How long have you been here?" He takes a bite of his sandwich.

"I was seven when I was adopted." I try to calm my racing heart.

"Your parents, they encouraged you to keep your language?" He leans back in his chair.

"My father spoke Russian, albeit poorly. His conversations made me laugh—he was constantly mixing up words—but they worked to keep me bi-lingual. What of your American family?" Normally I wouldn't pry, but he had.

He sips his tea before responding. "They encouraged me to speak English as much as possible and forget the past. But they didn't discourage me when my high school taught Russian. I thought it would be an easy A." His laugh deep and melodious like the summer wind in the mountains. "The grammar was my undoing. At the orphanage, they forced us to speak Russian, the 'language of unity.' I never learned it well. The Ukrainian I was taught at my mother's knee confused my verbs. There was nothing easy about that A."

For just a moment his smile reminds me of someone. The brightest spot in a dark place buried deep in my memory. A place

I'd rather not explore. "And your diction?" Stupid question, but my mind blanks.

"Flawless, although the teacher took issue with my accent." Again, he laughs, and my bright memory reappears. It has happened before: a Russian man, especially a handsome one, will, by his presence, open a window in that room I keep so tightly closed.

It is time I leave. I can't discuss the last five chapters of *War and Peace* with my students if I slip into my own melancholy. I put my book in my bag and make a show of checking my watch. "I really must go. It has been a pleasure."

True enough, not that we even exchanged names. He has enough information to find me if he wants to. I am the second youngest professor on campus and the only female who teaches Russian.

In an act of gallantry not seen in the cafeteria in over forty years, he stands before I can and helps me with my chair, then he holds my coat. I should offer my name.

I reach for my cane, my constant companion since I was three.

He looks away.

No, no names.

"Have a good day." I nod and wind through the maze of tables to the door where I toss my empty cup in the receptacle. He beats me to the door and holds it open for me.

"One more minute." He pleads in Russian.

What can I do? It's not as if I can prevent him from following me across campus. "If you can talk and walk." I gesture to the red and gray brick building at the far side of the quad.

"You remind me of a girl I grew up with. When her American parents came to take her away they brought a camera. I thought it the most wonderful thing. A Polaroid. They took a photo."

He holds out his phone.

I stumble.

He grabs my elbow.

I reach for his phone. Tears fill my eyes.

In the back of my closet, inside a scrapbook Mother made of

things of my life before, the twin to this photograph lies protected from time. "Mikhail?"

"Серце моє." A nickname I haven't heard in years, *my heart*, crosses his lips. His arms wrap around me as they had two decades ago. He's right: my heart is where it belongs.

I wonder what happens when the professor skips class.

SEVEN

CLOSING IN

Amanda Hill

"Aren't you ever going to leave?" I asked, hoping Gary could hear the fatigue in my voice. He turned away so I wouldn't see his eyes rolling, but I knew him too well. After Gary had taken a breath so he wouldn't say what he wanted to, he turned back around.

"Mom, just let me help. You still have a lot to unpack."

"I'm too tired." It wasn't my responsibility to soften the guilt he felt about forcing me into a senior care facility. As if helping me hang my clothes would make up for relegating me to the back of the closet like last year's sweater.

Not only was I being forced into a "home," he and his sisters were pushing me into this particular one with a director that made me uneasy. I couldn't explain it to my children, so they didn't listen. Now, I was here in the facility with the best value.

Value was critical because if I spent too much money, it would leave less for them in the end.

"That's why I need to stay and help. You relax, and I'll finish the work."

"You've done enough already." My words were clipped and terse.

Gary sighed, knowing it was pointless to argue with me. I might be old, but I was no pushover.

"How about a deal? I'll leave once I've introduced you to the neighbor across the hall."

I wanted him to leave without introductions, but he wouldn't make it that easy, so I didn't argue. At least he'd moved from patronizing to negotiating.

He didn't hide his eye roll as he left. If I wasn't going to be social, he was going to do it for me.

Willowbrook Estates was nothing like a real home. The prominent landscape paintings, plush chairs, and trendy decor didn't hide the easy-to-clean hard floors and neutral colors that would always remind a person of where they were. And all the air fresheners in the nearest big box store couldn't mask the smell of age.

He wasn't gone long before he came back with a hunched-back, old woman on his arm, smiling at her like she was a child. The way he smiles at me.

"Mom, this is Lona. Lona, this is my mother, Sharon." I smiled at the woman the same way Gary did and held out my hand. We exchanged pleasantries, and though she was quiet, she was alert.

"Would you like to join us for lunch?" Lona asked. "There's an extra seat at our table." She looked down to hide the choke in her voice. I'd never thought before how difficult it would be living in a place where friends were here one day gone the next. She recovered quickly and went on. "We like to call ourselves the ladies' club." She laughed to hide either her emotions or the terrible name of the club.

"Isn't that great mom? An invitation to lunch, and you're barely in the door." I gave him a look to remind him of his deal. One he couldn't miss.

"Well, you ladies have fun," he said. "I have to get back to Dana and the kids. I'll just walk you to the cafeteria, then get out of your hair."

"That shouldn't be difficult. We don't have much left," I said as I walked out the door.

———

The cafeteria and gathering area hadn't changed since the tour I'd taken weeks ago. A few small, round tables were next to couches and a fireplace. It was clean, but the smell of cafeteria food made it feel like an institution.

A dozen men and women sat at tables or in front of the TV, all of them waiting: waiting for visits, waiting for food, waiting for their favorite program, waiting to die.

Two men were yelling at the television, or each other, while a woman at a table in the corner sat so still, I wouldn't have been surprised if she were a wax figure. My morale dropped even lower as I realized that these were my new associates.

Lona grabbed my elbow and led me to the table. There were four seats, all open except one. Either we were early, or the group was smaller than I'd been led to believe. Had the woman in the corner been invited, or was she being shunned? Politics were everywhere, even in an old folk's home.

I was introduced to the woman at our table, Blanche. She smiled in my direction, but her eyes never focused on me, probably because she was frantically moving her hands in an original sign language only she knew. I waited for her to speak, but instead, she started spitting odd, jolting noises. I leaned away from her and gave Lona a questioning look.

"She's wrapping," Lona said.

"A gift?" I asked.

Lona laughed. "I don't mean wrapping a gift; I mean the music kind of rapping." She sat at her seat, and I followed suit. "Her grandson writes rap music, and he's the only one who comes to visit her. Besides, it's easier than trying to sing words at her age."

I'd never felt more isolated in my life.

Our odd group of three sat and talked of the weather, or two of us did while Blanche threw out one-word answers, among other weird noises, until a lunch worker brought our food in, and we became quiet. I was in the worst ladies' club on the planet.

Lona tried to drum up more conversation. "Blanche, don't you think Sharon's jewelry is beautiful?"

I wasn't surprised my matching set of earrings and bracelet caught her attention; they were more expensive than an entire month's rent in my suite. Staying here wasn't cheap, and I was in the biggest room. I'd always enjoyed having money until it became something my children coveted.

"Mm-hmm," was all Blanche replied. She did at least look at the earrings before going back to her soup.

Lona couldn't stand up straight or walk without a walker, but she was the only one with any conversation skills.

"So, Lona, what brought you here?"

She looked confused and took a sip of her tea before responding.

"As I said before, I fell down the stairs trying to get to the laundry room in the basement. I broke my hip, and the doctor said I shouldn't live alone anymore."

The last of my hope sunk. Lona couldn't carry a normal conversation like I'd thought, any more than the others. Her memory must not be what it seemed.

I skipped over her lapse, determined to find out what I wanted. "But surely bones heal," I replied. "You're sharper than ..." I paused, unsure how to say it tactfully, "some of the others around us. Is it possible for you to leave at some point?"

She gave me a confused look again, probably a regular facial expression for her. "It was less about my hip bone healing and more a concern of what would happen the next time I fell."

"But what if you could strengthen your hip and prove you don't belong here? Is there not a way out?"

She gave me that smile, the one she would save for a child, put her hand over mine, and said, "We'd all love to leave, but there's only one way out of here."

———

I didn't see the director often, the only bright spot in my new life. Lona and the nurses were my only real companions. I had quite a few nurses, but one came more often than the others. Her name was Elise, and she had a British accent, which made her sound altogether too cheery.

"You're too rough," I told her one day when she was checking my vitals. "I know how tight an arm pressure cuff should go, and you're taking it too far." I was sure she was trying to make me faint.

"Sorry," she replied. She didn't sound like she meant it.

The flowers Gary left on my nightstand stood between us. "Lovely flowers, Sharon. Should I tuck them in over here?" Without waiting for a response, she picked up the pot of lilies and walked toward the windowsill.

"No, you may not," I said. My voice left no room for argument. Elise needed to learn she couldn't patronize me or order me around.

She stopped mid-stride at my outburst.

"You think I shouldn't decide where to keep my flowers because I'm old?"

"I didn't say …"

I cut her off. "You have no right to treat me like a child, and I demand you leave this instant."

She smiled at me, more a display of her teeth, and set the pot back where it had been. "Sorry to upset you, Sharon. I'll check one more thing and be on my way."

I still knew how to command a situation.

———

Over time, I met new people and was treated with contempt and disrespect by the staff and residents alike. On the few occasions I saw Director Daphne, she smiled like a wolf, and I escaped as fast I could. I still had an odd feeling about her, and I couldn't shake it.

I tried to be friendly. Once, I explained to another resident that if she used a boar bristle brush instead of a cheap one, her hair wouldn't look so greasy. And I mentioned to another that if she wanted others to listen to her, she shouldn't shout so loud. Instead of taking my advice, they treated me like a pariah. I was just trying to help.

Time went on, residents took meals, old men yelled, and Blanche rapped. Boredom crept into the edges of my despair. I tried retail therapy, my cure for everything in the past, but I couldn't go shopping unless my children took me and that rarely happened. They'd all stopped by for visits, but it was never long before they checked their watches, or their phones pinged, and they made apologies for having to leave so soon.

Online ordering was an option, but it wasn't the same. Still, it was all I had, so I spent much of my time browsing my favorite online boutiques, trying to convince myself it helped.

Many of the residents shied away from technology, but it was no mystery to me. You couldn't be in my line of work without knowing your way around a computer, and I would never be caught asking my children or grandchildren for help with technology. The gall of an entire generation thinking they were smarter than the parents who raised them was beyond me.

I was in the middle of one of my pointless online shopping sprees at the technology center when Lona walked in with a sour expression on her face.

"Who do they think they are, pushing me around like that?"

"Who was pushing you around?"

Her response was a grumble I couldn't understand, but I did hear the word "nurses." It must have been Elise.

"What did she do?"

Lona grumbled again but ignored me. She may not have wanted to talk about it, but she was right. They shouldn't treat us this way. Didn't we have laws to protect us? Had no one complained before?

The thought made my mind go into planning mode, with ideas of cameras, traps, and stake-outs running rampant. I'd retired years ago, and I was too old to pull something like that off, by myself, no less, but I still thought about it. I'd been an excellent private investigator, but the thought of that much work now made me tired.

I went to my room, took my shoes off, and glanced at the

dresser, surprised to see my bracelet sitting on top, alone without the matching earrings.

I'd worn them together, took them off together, and put them on the dresser together. I knew I had. I went to get a closer look, reprimanding myself on the way for not putting them in the safe where they belonged, but it was too late now. Getting a closer look confirmed my suspicions. Someone had taken them.

I wondered why someone would take only the earrings and not the bracelet. If the thief knew their value, they would have taken both. It had to have been someone who wanted the jewelry, not what they could get for them. I remembered my first meal here and Lona's comments. She was the only person who'd ever noticed the earrings or took any interest in them.

The stolen jewelry made napping impossible, which in turn made it harder to think. My mind jumped from one problem to another, unable to land on a solution. My children had stashed me here, the staff was abusive, and Lona had stolen my earrings. The world needed saving, and no superheroes were on the horizon.

I went to the kitchen to get coffee despite the late hour. I needed more clarity of mind and didn't care if it was going to keep me up. It didn't matter when I slept or didn't sleep anyway. No one cared.

A bobble-head Hawaiian dancer swayed her hips on the coffee counter, and I thought of a time I'd worked in Hawaii and watched real Hawaiian dancers. This care facility was like the bobble-head; a tiny, fake version of real life. It gave me an idea.

I stopped stirring and almost dropped my mug. I set it down and put my hand to my forehead. Why hadn't I thought of this before? I couldn't pull off a major operation, but that didn't mean I couldn't do something smaller.

Shopping online with a purpose was much more fun than shopping to pass the time. I spent all that evening and the next morning researching covert cameras, from speakers to smoke detectors and smaller options like buttons and pens. I giggled as I imagined myself walking around the lounge, holding a pen in the air, trying to act nonchalant.

After much consideration, I settled on an alarm clock camera. I couldn't put one up in the main areas; I'd be found out. And putting one in Lona's room was crossing a line I didn't want to cross yet, so my room was where I'd have to start. I could catch Elise's abuse and have evidence when Lona stole more of my things.

Who would suspect an old woman of owning and operating an alarm clock camera? It was genius. Underestimation could be my new superpower. I clicked the "purchase" button and felt like a hero in a crime drama. All I needed now was patience.

―――――

After the longest week of my life, the alarm clock arrived. It looked like any other alarm clock except for the SD card slot in the back. As long as it was plugged in, it would record for 12 hours before recording over previous footage. The camera could be turned on and off with the touch of a button, and the set up was easy enough that some of my new friends could have figured it out.

I left my room as often as possible, giving ample opportunity for anyone to come and take whatever they wanted. When I had to be with the nurses, I was especially difficult, looking for a reaction. There were a few times I thought I'd caught something incriminating, but when I went back to watch the footage, it looked different than I'd remembered. But it was only a matter of time. I had a hard time hiding my impatience and excitement, and at dinner, Lona commented on it.

"Sharon, you look different lately. Almost happy, like you're anticipating a party."

My back stiffened, and I glared at her. "Don't I usually look happy?" I scoffed. "What are you getting at?"

She thought a second before speaking. "Well, usually, you look like you're hiding a cactus in your pants."

I gasped in outrage, stood up, and threw my napkin on my seat. "I won't sit here another minute listening to you ridicule me. You're no better than a common thief." I paused to see if she'd take the bait, but she was too stunned to speak. I knew I shouldn't give her anything more, but I couldn't hold my tongue any longer. "I know you stole my earrings, and I can prove it!"

Her eyes widened in mock surprise, but I stalked off before she could carry her innocent act any further. Let her stew on that.

———

I went to the technology center; I had nothing better to do. I watched more footage but found nothing. Living your life, then watching it a second time, even in fast motion, was painfully dull.

Lona and I kept our distance for a few days, but there weren't many places to go to avoid each other. One morning when I was watching the monotony of my video feed, Lona sat at the only available computer, the one next to me. She was talking to herself, muttering on about life not being so bad if she only had the freedom to leave. The more she spoke, the louder she got, and soon I wasn't sure if she was talking to herself or me.

"Being here looks great on paper. We have food, social lives, medical attention, and activities, but we're no different than criminals, imprisoned in jail."

She was right. Still a thief, but a correct thief. Though I wasn't ready to get over my anger, I had to admit we shared the same fate.

"Well then, I say we leave," I said.

Lona laughed, which sounded more like a cough, and though I wasn't joking, I laughed too.

"We can't do that," she said.

"Why not?"

"The door codes for one."

My recent covert operations made me confident, the lack of

activity on my feed made me bored, and the two combined made me reckless. "Aren't we smarter than door codes?"

"I don't know if I'm smarter than a door, let alone one with codes."

"Maybe you aren't, but I am. Can you create a distraction?"

———

The fire alarm produced less panic than I'd hoped. Too many drills and false alarms made everyone shake their heads and wish they didn't have to lose twenty minutes of their day.

Lona had played her part well. They didn't trust us with real kitchen equipment, but there was still a toaster, and I could smell burnt bread.

It took the office staff a full sixty seconds to voice their complaints and shuffle outside. I knew because I counted, biding my time in the public restroom across the hall until it was quiet. The caretakers would be doing a sweep of the building to make sure all residents were out, but they'd start with the less mobile. If I had luck on my side, I'd be done and out before anyone came looking for me.

When the hall was empty besides an old man walking in circles yelling, "Take cover! Save yourself!" I decided it was as clear as it was going to get, so I crossed to the office.

The first computer was the secretary's, and it was an excellent place to start. The screen was still unlocked. Security wasn't much of a concern when surrounded by the elderly. I wasn't a hacker, but using a basic search function usually did the trick if someone wasn't trying to hide something, and I found the file for the door codes right away. It was too easy.

My excitement didn't last long when I clicked on the file, and a prompt for a password popped up. I tried all the obvious ones, including the address for Willowbrook, with no success. There wasn't much time, and it was running out fast. I should have put more preparation into our scheme. Why was I making rookie mistakes? If I hadn't been so eager, I would have figured out her birthday, or that of her children's. If underestimation was my superpower, overconfidence was my weakness. Lona and I would have to regroup and try again later.

I was about to go outside to waste my twenty minutes with the rest of the facility when I saw a folder labeled "medical files" and clicked on it. My name was listed alphabetically with the other residents. I was afraid and curious at the same time, but curiosity won out. It was probably password locked anyway, so I clicked on it.

The file opened right away. Door codes had to be on lockdown but not personal information? What kind of security was this?

Doctor's notes and health records stared back at me, and though I knew I didn't want to see, I couldn't look away. My children had convinced my doctor of 20 years to diagnose me with dementia despite a lack of conclusive evidence. All he had was stories my children told about me being forgetful or blaming others for my problems. All lies. They were the forgetful ones.

They ran tests, ones the doctors admitted weren't perfect, yet still, they diagnosed me and took everything from me. In the end, I think it was the fact that people would rather believe sensational stories over boring truth.

I'd had enough and was about to leave when Director Daphne walked into the office. I froze, caught by the wolf, with nowhere to hide. I could yell, but everyone was outside. Why wasn't she outside? She must have waited for this moment when we'd be alone together, and now she was closing in. What made me think I was still cut out for this?"

I was about to scream, whether someone could hear or not, when she spoke in a high-pitched, sing-song voice, "Did you get lost?"

Her words cut through my panic, making me breathe easier. I'd forgotten my power of underestimation, and I'd never felt more thankful for it. I was sure she had schemes up her sleeve, but as long as she didn't think I was a threat, I could pass by unnoticed. I knitted my brows together and looked around, hoping I looked confused enough. "Isn't this where we're supposed to go?"

She smiled, took my hand, and said, "Come on, I'll walk you out."

———

It was cold outside. The staff said it felt good compared to the sauna inside, but they were crazy. I tried not to think about the words from my medical file, staring me in the face as I waited, but they wouldn't go away.

We didn't succeed with the door codes, but we didn't get caught either. Lona and I would try again when we were better prepared, and it would work. I started thinking through details in my mind when I saw Lona walking out of the building, pushing her walker. I hadn't realized she was still inside. Curious, since she was the one to set the alarm off. I expected her to be the first one out, despite her walker. Maybe she'd wanted to stay warm indoors as long as she could, knowing there wasn't any real danger, but it did seem odd.

It didn't take long for the director to clear the building and let us back in. No private investigator was needed to see a toaster caused the alarm. I was left to walk in on my own since others needed more help than I did. Before I got far, Blanche grabbed my hand and placed something soft inside. A bright dandelion. We locked eyes for a moment before she let go and walked away. I looked at the flower, then at her retreating form. The last time someone gave me a dandelion, it was a child.

I was in a circus, but I was the only spectator, surrounded by oddities.

I went straight to my room, dropped the flower on the dresser, and sat on the bed when something caught the corner of my eye. I turned and stared, stunned, at my missing earrings on the bedpost. How had they gotten there?

I wasted no time turning to my alarm clock and taking out the SD card. Lona was smarter than I gave her credit. Here I thought I was planning a great coup while she'd been planning a better one all along. My confrontation must have rattled her and scared her into returning my earrings. She knew I'd be out of my room, and no one would be paying her any attention. It would have been perfect if I hadn't had a camera.

At the technology center, I slipped the card into the computer and waited. Why did it have to be so slow? I watched the video in fast motion until I saw movement in the room and slowed it to regular speed, but instead of Lona, it was a nurse checking for an occupant. I choked out a laugh when she checked under the bed. Did she think I was limber enough to hide under there?

Now that the evidence of Lona's thievery was within my grasp, I knew it wouldn't be long before I had proof of the mistreatment of the staff. They'd have no choice but to listen to me then, and I could prove I didn't have dementia. I was closing in, and I'd walk out of here by the end of the week.

The nurse left the room, and I sped the recording up as fast as I dared, watching, holding my breath until I saw someone else come in. My fingers moved to slow the video down, but before I could, the screen went blank and turned off.

I was the one who'd walked in.

I started the video over again, and this time didn't speed it up. I had to have missed something and would have to watch carefully to catch it. The minutes in real-time moved like the minutes of life, dragging on before slipping away. I watched a second time as the nurse came in, looked under the bed, then left.

My eyes toggled from the room on the screen to the countdown at the bottom. Forty seconds left for Lona to come in. She had to have moved fast. 35 seconds. So quick, I missed her the first time. 30 seconds. It wouldn't take long to walk in, drop the earrings, then leave. 25 seconds. Any time now. 20 seconds. I was beginning to despair. 15 seconds. Was that movement I saw? I knew time was slipping away too fast, but I couldn't face it. I watched myself walk into the room, drop the flower, look at the bedpost, pick up the earrings, then turn off the camera.

Lona never came.

I didn't remember walking back, but I ended up in bed, thinking. I'd pulled off more successful operations in my career than I could count, and now I couldn't find door codes, catch a thief, or get my life back. My skills were failing me when I needed them most.

I jumped when Elise knocked, coming into the room to check on me.

"How are you feeling today, Sharon?"

I didn't answer her. I didn't have to talk to her. Who was she to think she could come at any time she wanted and require me to play hostess? My silence didn't bother her, she poked, prodded, and checked my breathing while trying to make conversation. All I wanted was for her to leave so I could be alone with my thoughts until she mentioned my earrings. I hadn't realized I'd been staring at them.

"They're so lovely." Her words ripped me out of my thoughts. "I notice them every time I come in to check on you. You might want to put them somewhere safe so they don't get lost."

I hadn't heard anything after the words, 'every time.'

"How long have they been there?" I asked, casually.

"Since the day you got here. I noticed you wearing them, and they've been on the bedpost since." The arm pressure cuff expanded, tightening on my arm, tensing my whole body. "I thought it was an odd place to put them, but who am I to suggest how you arrange your room?" She winked at me, and I wanted to poke out that winking eye.

I felt like yelling and screaming, letting her know she was wrong. I hadn't put the earrings there. I would have remembered. I wouldn't have forgotten I'd put them there. I wouldn't have blamed Lona for stealing. I wouldn't have missed them sitting on the post for days.

Would I?

I could find out. I still had hours of footage from my room; I could go back and watch. I could prove the earrings hadn't been there the whole time, or ...

I didn't want to admit even to myself what I might find instead. If I'd been wrong about this, could I have been wrong about everything else? The arm pressure cuff was cutting off my circulation, blackening my vision, turning my heart into a brick. My world was closing in. I tried to tell Elise she was killing me, but no words came out.

The cuff finally relaxed, allowing oxygen back into my brain and blood back into my heart, but neither banished the fear. I knew I couldn't face watching video surveillance ever again.

Elise finished her work and left.

In the silence, I looked at the flower on my nightstand. Clean, sharp, full of life, but in the morning, it would already begin fading, showing signs of age it could never get back.

What if I wasn't so different from Lona, or Blanche, or the loud old men? What if I belonged here? But it couldn't be. My intelligence was my identity. If I didn't have my mind, what did I have?

Who am I, if I am no longer me?

EIGHT

AIN'T NO WATER IN THE PIPES

Denis Feehan

"It's been fifty years now, but it seems like only yesterday," my grand-father told me.

"Oh boy," I thought, "here we go again."

Grandpa sat up straighter in his wheelchair. "We woke up that morning to the sound of my momma screaming for Daddy. 'Henry, it's happened! We ain't got no water!' My sister and I jumped up and run to the kitchen. Sure enough, there was Momma, standing at the sink, dressed in the green and white robe that she had worn every day of my seven years on this earth, staring at the water tap. It was turned wide open but just as dry as a camel's mouth two miles from an oasis."

Grandpa continued with the story that I had heard a hundred times before. "Poppa ran out to the field to check the water for the crops. Our well had been dry for a week already but the county's irrigation pipes had still been spitting out enough water for our crops. Until that day."

I sank deeper in my chair. This was going to take twenty-two minutes and thirty-one seconds. I knew the exact time because I had clocked it the last time he told me the story. Which was only last week, on Wednesday, when my mom dropped me off for my weekly visit to Grandpa's house while she went to the PTA meeting.

"Let me guess," I thought. "The whole town was dry."

"But you know what?" he said. "We found out the whole town was dry. Now, the Mayor had been warning us that the water reserves was all gone but he was cat sure that he could trade some of our wheat to Franklin City for a week's worth of water."

I thought, "Maybe I should ask him about the game last night. Try to change the subject."

But Grandpa was on a roll. "Had no luck in Franklin City. They was nearly out theirselves. The mayor called a meetin' of our city council, but the whole dang town showed up. First meetin' I ever saw without water pitchers on the tables for the councilmen. Anyhow, they told us that our water was all gone, like we hadn't already knowed that. Told us that the mayor had called the governor to get some water shipped in."

I knew what Grandpa would say next: "Gonna take a few days what with the weather ... "

And Grandpa said, "But it was gonna take a few days what with the weather up in these mountains. Well, sir, it took a week to get any water and even then it weren't enough to help with the crops. Just some drinkin' water. And then you know what happened?"

"Riots, Grandpa?" Like I didn't know, I thought.

"Yer darn tootin' riots. Some folks was stealing other folks' water to put on their crops. Others was stealin' the water just to sell it. A water bottle ain't got no ID on it so no one knew if they was buyin' back their own water. Which they was."

"Some of them hobos what bunk down by the creek bed, which was as dry as a desert on the Fourth of July, come into town and broke into old man Sherrill's store. The water was all gone, of course, so they started shovin' cupcakes and candy bars in their pockets. Sheriff Saunders heard the alarm and he and Deputy Conner arrested the lot of 'em.

"Pretty soon some folks was loadin' up to protect what little they had. One thing led to another and a couple of those Deeken boys got theirselves killed."

"Did they have to call the National Guard, Grandpa?"

"Well, as a matter of fact they did. The guard come in and was able to establish order. Two days later it started raining. Rained for seven straight days and truth be told, we ain't had a lick of water trouble for the last fifty years."

"Great story, Grandpa. Can we have the ice cream now?"

"You bet. Comin' right up."

"Do you have rocky road?"

"Well, now, you know I do!"

———

That was three days ago. Today, I'm sitting in this freezing cold church next to my mom. I can hear her crying, but I can't see her tears behind the black veil.

Grandpa told me that big boys don't cry. So, staring at the coffin, with the bouquet of red roses from his garden draped over the middle, I'm biting my lip and wishing that I could hear that story just one more time.

NINE

I WAS NOT THERE, YET I WAS THERE

Brenda Birch Gallaher

I was not there, yet...I was there. As I lay in the hospital bed, tubes were stuck in me everywhere. They were useless. My soul had already left my body, and I watched from the only empty spot in the room. It was the far corner. My daddy had taken the awkward-looking recliner and moved it over to the side of my bed, and this is where he sat—night and day—as he waited for me to open my eyes.

I felt sorry for my daddy. He had five boys and one girl. I was that girl. The one child who never caused him any grief. I was a solid B student with a few A's sprinkled in. I was the one he taught to fish, catch balls, and curse like a sailor. But mine weren't real curse words—they were made up. My mother would have never allowed her only daughter to speak in such a manner.

But none of that mattered now. His little sailor-swearing princess lay in a hospital bed—brain dead. I had seen my father cry only once before my accident, and that was when his twin sister died. I was ten years old. It was hard for me to comprehend his sorrow and pain. I loved my brothers but could not understand the concept of one of them dying, therefore, I could not understand my father's grief over the loss of his sister. It wasn't until my mother died when I was fifteen that I finally understood how the pain of losing a loved one could actually grip my heart, making me lose my breath. Daddy hid his tears at his eternal companion's death.

Every day, for the past week, my father sat in that awful chair, held my hand and sniffled. I was aware of his presence but could not respond, not even when he squeezed my hand. I was 25 now, and that's all I would ever be. A young woman, cut down in the prime of her life by a drunk driver. In essence, I was murdered. Now that my soul had left my body, I could observe my father from a distance. His head hung, he cried, and he never let go of my hand. Several times I saw a nurse or orderly come to my room door, look at my father, shake their head, and leave. She had told him to take his time and sit with me for as long as he liked. This was after the doctor came in and told him there was no hope—I was gone.

My internal organs were so destroyed by the other car t-boning me that I couldn't even be a donor. My father would have granted my wishes, but it would not have made him happy. It would have been one more grief piled upon another, and it was not something he needed. Three of my brothers had come to see me. One had died in the car accident on impact, and the other one died when my mother did.

I looked over my shoulder and upwards. Why was I surprised I could hear my younger brother calling me? I didn't want to go. I wasn't ready to go. I wasn't ready to leave my father. He was sad as it was, but losing two children at once must be just as bad as when he lost Mother and Charlie. Bobby would just have to wait while I stayed with Daddy. He needs someone with him while he mourns.

I placed my hand on my father's shoulder, but he did not move nor acknowledge my touch. How could he? I was gone. But I wasn't gone. I was still in this room with Daddy. I could still think. I could still feel. I could still love. Without my consent, my soul began to move towards the ceiling. I don't want to go. I want to stay. Soon, as I moved further away from the life I knew, Daddy moved further away from me. I was not there, yet…I was there.

TEN

SEMPER FI: THE MARINE WIFE

C.H. Lindsay

The Marine next door
    dressed in camouflage
    walks past the window.
    "Dada!" my one-year-old calls.
    But it's not Daddy.
    It can't be Daddy.
    Not today,
    not her birthday,
    not this Christmas.

When he returns,
    we'll talk
    of honor,
    of duty,
    of freedom.
    But now,
    I hold her close,
    and cry,
    and wait

for the right Marine
to walk past the window.

ELEVEN

THREE WEEKS TO THE DAY

Elizabeth Watson Barnes

Days of not sweeping, maybe weeks, maybe years, and suddenly it's all she wants to do. Maybe it's the gentle repeated sound of bristles against the floor, like waves repeating or simply that the broom handle steadies her and gives her something to hold on to, whatever it is, she gives what remains to sweeping.

In every room (did you hear what I said? In *every room!*) she sweeps up at least one, sometimes two or three tiny round rubber elastics.

It is unexpected.

These elastics. (My knees buckle.)

The dog hair and dust bunnies make a nest for them. She rushes from room to room, her mouth gaping and her breathing coming too fast. There are not enough broom handles in the world.

"Those those those those." Staccato until they bleed into nothing and her lips stay shaped in an 'O'. (Her elastics...*hers!*)

She stops moving.

I walk towards her, and the breeze I make sends dog hair floating and twirling across the floor. She quickly reaches out with the broom and pulls things back into place around the elastics and then forgets again that I am here.

A phone buzzes, and because random things have been taken over by the autonomic nervous system, she reaches for it and stares.

Text Message:

This is a reminder from Dawson Pediatric Dentistry and Orthodontics:
    You have an appointment on Tuesday at 1:00.
    Please press 'Y' to confirm 'N' to cancel.

(The tiny elastics.)

She makes a sound that I have never heard before and hits 'N' so hard the phone falls to the floor and rattles.

"Tuesday." she whispers to no one. I nod.

(Exactly three weeks to the day.)

Her brain inhales and pauses. Her eyes flutter.

I turn off the phone.

Morning comes, and she is surprised. There is nothing to do but make a breakfast and wait. She spoons scrambled eggs into her mouth faster than she can swallow, choking and sputtering, and she can't get enough of anything and grabs the toast and can't chew it fast enough. Milk spills down her front and she looks around and there is nothing heavy enough or sharp enough or enough enough. (I am here love, I am right here.)

She is sitting on the wooden chair when the food comes back up and lands heavy and warm in her empty lap. She heaves and gasps and lets me put my arm around her (she is as skinny as a child, and I start to cry). She lets me help her to her feet (my heart) and lead her to the bathroom. I slip her nightgown off her shoulders and the weight of the mess drops it to the floor. She shivers. I wrap her in a towel and start the shower. She is standing there, clutching the towel, her head bowed, surrounded by steam (heartbreakingly beautiful). She is unsteady, barely able to lift her legs over the edge of the tub. She is still gripping the towel, her fingers white. The water hits the back of her neck, and she moans but doesn't lift her head, the soaked towel is too heavy now, it is all too heavy and she lets it slip from her hands. She folds at the waist (oh god!). Her head hits the buttons on my shirt, hot water fills my shoes. She leans. I press my lips to her wet hair.

(I need to say something, and I'm going to whisper it. If I don't say it I may never hear it again. I need to hear it again. I need to say it in italics, slanted to the right like her head when she laughed and it needs to smell like grape Hubba Bubba bubble gum and knock-knock jokes and kite string and it needs to be in the center of everything.)

Emeree

We are beyond crying. The water has turned cold. Her body is pressed against mine, arms limp to her side. We manage our way to the bedroom. (I can't stop shaking.)

She pulls free of my hand and falls toward the bed in a rush. I pull the tucked bedspread from either side and wrap her tight. She frees an arm and grabs my hand and squeezes hard and in minutes she is asleep and I am still soaking wet and holding her hand.

Hours or days later I am wrapped in bed with her and finally warm. I hear the knock, and I am instantly angry. I don't want to leave her. I slip on my robe and almost shut the bedroom door behind me. (I am afraid if she wakes up alone she will forget me again.)

It's her mother. She has something covered in foil and a determined look on her face. Wants to know where her daughter is, wants to know why I am not dressed, why no one is answering the phone, we can't just lock ourselves away, we aren't the only ones who are sad, who are grieving. (But not like this, no one else, like this.)

She pelts me with words and marches through the house. She heads for the bedroom. I block her path. She veers into the study as if it was her idea and steps right on it.

The pile. The nest. The tiny elastics.

(I make a sound I have never heard before.)

She follows my eyes to the floor and shakes her head. Mutters something under her breath and heads for the broom and dustpan. I am dangerous. (I will wrestle her if I have to, I will growl and snarl and drop to all fours spitting and howling and weeping.)

I tell her she needs to go and her eyes flash hot and I will not back down this time or ever again. Words are said. Loudly. I hustle her out the door and lock it. She stands on the porch stunned.

I hurry to the bedroom, and my love is clinging to the door, half in half out. She has heard everything. I tighten my robe and take a deep breath.

"You kicked her out."

"Yes."

She nods and looks at me like it's twenty years ago.

"Thank you."

Her words come rushing now and she grips the door with her hand to keep from crumbling and I want to go to her but her voice pins me to the floor. It is coming in waves, the words, soaking both of us with all the things she won't ever do or see or feel...our daughter, Emeree, and the boys she won't date and the trips she won't take and she should have let her get her ears pierced and what about Christmas and college and the man she won't marry and the children the children the children she won't have and we are both sobbing and she is in my arms and we are holding each other. Each. Other.

Suddenly she stops crying and wipes her nose on my robe.

"Where's Piper?" (The reason for the dog hair.)

"Next door, it was just too hard...with everything."

"We have to go get her. Emeree would want her here." (Her name, our beautiful daughter's name.)

"Of course, of course."

We dress quickly and rush through the house and to the back door. Behind us, dust bunnies and dog hair swirl and drift and fall gently to the floor, cradling Emeree's tiny elastics.

TWELVE

IRENE KENDALL NEVER EXISTED

Robin Glassey

When I googled Irene Kendall today, I couldn't find her. There were no articles or images . . . certainly no social media accounts. In the eyes of the world, Irene's not rich, famous, or influential. It's as though she doesn't exist.

Never existed.

For a woman who always shied away from cameras, crowds, and didn't even tell her mother about her school graduation so she wouldn't have to attend, Irene has changed my life and the lives of countless people.

Three weeks ago, I visited my 100-year-old grandmother in a care center. Her stuttered crying escaped into the hall as I approached her room. Franny—as everyone calls her—no longer recognizes anyone. I'm a stranger to her.

As I entered Franny's room, drab light from an overcast day filtered through the window, passing over a pile of photo albums of grandchildren and great-grandchildren before coming to rest on her gaunt figure. Franny's head poked above her purple afghan, her cheekbones protruding from her face, her grey pixie haircut unchar-acteristically disheveled.

Her rheumy eyes lacked a brightness, that hint of humor, that

flash of fire which had earned her another nickname—Frambo—
after the gun-toting character, Rambo.

My mother claimed Franny's time has almost come.

Perhaps.

She's fooled us many times when she's been on the "brink of
death" only to rally again. You can't tell Frambo what to do. Only
she decides. And if you ask my husband, he'll tell you that's a gift I
got from Franny.

My jaw tightened. My throat constricted. I realized my mother
was right. There would be no rallying this time.

I searched for some sign that Franny recognized me, but she
babbled incessantly—stringing nonsense syllables together in a
language only she understood. After a minute, two words sliced
cleanly through the river of dementia:

"Go away."

Had I imagined it?

But she repeated, "Go away, go away, go away."

Hurt clawed up.

I stamped it out.

When it comes to memory, dementia is a cruel smash-and-grab
thief with no discretion.

But honestly, Franny never was a cuddly, cookie-baking kind of
grandmother. She was more of a hug and release, cookie-buying
kind of grandmother who sprinkled love on my ice cream with
crushed-up cookies.

I remember more about Franny's house than I do about time
spent with her in it. Her home fascinated me with its plastic-cup
chandelier, miniature glass figurines, and wigged Styrofoam heads—
featureless sentinels that sat on the shelf of her genealogy room.
The disembodied reminders of my grandmother guarded the
doorway saying, "Look but don't enter."

Even Franny's kitchen table piqued my curiosity. Small bowls
held every paperclip and rubber band she'd ever found along with
pencils, pens, pennies, and more. The table stood as a monument to
lessons learned from surviving the Great Depression, WWII, and
the early death of her spouse.

Franny scrimped her whole life, but any extra she willingly gave, doing it without fanfare—the living embodiment of the widow's mite. I survived my first two semesters of BYU thanks to Franny. And it was during that second semester at BYU that I began dating the man I ended up marrying.

My debt to Franny extends further, however. In 1954, Franny met missionaries from The Church of Jesus Christ of Latter-day Saints. After investigating for two years, Franny gave up ironing with her iron in one hand and a beer in the other and was baptized. When she met "Butch," the pool-hustler her youngest daughter was dating, Franny's member-missionary efforts began in earnest.

But how does a woman who saves every penny and rubber band change the lives of *countless* people? Doctrine & Covenants 14:7 proposes that eternal life is the greatest of all the gifts of God. How many souls have access to God's gift of eternal life simply because of Franny's one decision in 1956 to be baptized? I've lost track.

Franny's posterity has served missions worldwide in places such as Ukraine, England, and Madagascar, and in even more strange and unusual places like Tennessee, Idaho, and Arizona. Some individuals they have taught and baptized have also served missions.

Franny herself was the first missionary in our family and one of the first Canadian sisters in The Church of Jesus Christ of Latter-day Saints called to the Washington D.C. Temple. Despite depression, anxiety, health challenges and more, she's endured all things put in her path and carried on.

Franny often told me: *"Like my co-worker at Laura Secords used to say when work was less than easy, 'Cheer up, things could be worse,' So we cheered up and sure enough, things got worse. Then we would have a good laugh over the whole situation and carry on."*

———

I stood in Franny's room, knowing this would be my last moment with her. My last earthly goodbye, at least. "I love you, Franny."

Years of love and sweet memories spilled out the corners of my eyes.

Since that visit, things have taken a turn for the worse. This morning, one of my sisters messaged me saying there might not be a funeral service, but rather a quick graveside service. I panicked. Would Franny leave this life as quietly and unrecognized as she'd lived it?

No!

The world might not care who Irene Kendall is, but I do. Franny's life and legacy have been one of quiet dedication and service to her family—both living and dead—and to her God. Of carrying on. Who can measure her worth? Who can measure her influence?

I can't measure it, but I experience Franny's influence each day as I teach my sons that same gospel of Jesus Christ that she accepted back in 1956. That one choice in the past is my present and my future.

For this great gift and more, I celebrate, honor, and remember Irene Kendall.

*Addendum: Irene Kendall returned to her heavenly home on May 7, 2019, a week after this was originally written.

THIRTEEN

METHOD TO MADNESS

Marie Tollstrup

Dad's question hangs high like ripened grapes, a sweet allure. What will you be grown up? We play sleight-of-hand cards, holding *priest with collar* or *nun in habit*. Rather, we reach to pluck the fruit of romantic travel away from home. I hear *the call* to be saved. Dad sculpts a blessing on my forehead, and I travel to a convent universe. A host of girls, thirteen to fourteen sign up, gain an endorphin high by serving others and dying to self like monks of old, feasting on idealism.

The church invites the uninitiated: girls who never dated with intent and reticent to touch flesh on flesh, girls, supple as saplings, who bend to Superior's whimsical winds known for her rosary sleight-of-hand, naïve girls who never savored life, programmed to persevere as nuns till death. How long can will and sexuality be denied? The seed sprouts, not heeding boundaries. Desires spill forth, ooze with maturity. Starved of touch, choice, friendship, I bolt for a tactile, wider world and relish freedom from youth-vows to seek the sweet allure of ripened grapes, madness stamped on my every move.

FOURTEEN

FROM FEAR TO FAITH

Valarie Schenk

I grew up scared to explore matters of faith. Mom displayed religious relics around our home, but as a topic of discussion, these items were dismissed. A curious girl, I stood entranced in front of them: the print of a man with clasped hands (warm eyes and graying head), the concealed crucifix hanging in her bedroom, and the framed blessing written in cryptic Norse. Transfixed, frozen, I remained hopelessly drawn to the secrets they guarded. I couldn't leave them alone. Curiosity, mixed with thick shame, bubbled deep within. I pined for the times that Mom left me home alone which provided opportunities for closer investigation.

Each time her car turned the corner down the street, I habitually darted down the basement stairs and rushed, adrenaline pumping, into her room. My trembling hands retrieved the crucifix off the bent nail that held it snug against the cold wall. Its shape remained a crisscrossed silhouette on the yellowed wallpaper – a delicate lace print interwoven with tiny blush roses. Timidly, I slid the crucifix open, not knowing the significance of the man that adorned its face. Entombed in its carved recesses slept two candles, white, pristine, unburned. I reasoned that the two indents found on right and left sides held the candles and slipped them into place, a perfect fit. Ceremonial instructions were included on thin, crisp paper. The words they held, however, remained dead to me, incomprehensible. I imagined they must be bad, and if not bad then sacred, and, therefore, not meant for me. Scared my lingering might conjure evil spirits, I became adept at re-folding the unread papers to bury them snugly in their wooden grave.

I reverently moved next, always, to the cabinet that encased family photo albums . . . also off limits. Cross-legged and lost in time, I reverently flipped through pages of familiar and not-so-familiar faces. The ritual was short. Mom was never gone long. I expertly replaced each item in its respective home, swallowed the guilt, and carried on with my day.

Mom and Dad dutifully ensured that my sister and I were baptized into the Lutheran Church, a faith neither of them practiced, to appease Grandma and Grandpa. More relics were collected and stashed with "hands off" valuables. Soon to follow was a personal Bible, a gift from Grandma with hopes that faith would be firmly planted. As was custom with topics of religion, those events were pushed aside. But, the Bible was a magnet. I read from it, protected within the confines of my bedroom closet, door closed, darkened, with flashlight in hand. I was terrified of being caught, of being made fun of, of being misunderstood. Like an addict lured by drugs, I felt ashamed and kept my doings hidden.

The only prayer I remember offering as a child was with my sister. We huddled on my bed, covered ourselves with a heavy bed spread, clicked on a cassette recorder and uttered with suppressed giggles our prayer into a microphone. We asked our "dear Heavenly Father" (Was He really there? Was that really His name?) about the weather and other such trivial matters. I vaguely remember closing the prayer with a resolute "Amen." After my sister left, I played the recording over and over again.

I yearned for religion. Permission to explore it, I perceived, was not granted.

Years later, as a college student, I found myself empty, fearful about the future, and grappling for answers. On a particularly low day, I received a letter in the mail from my closest friend, Mike, who was then serving as a missionary in Brazil for The Church of Jesus Christ of Latter-day Saints. Early in the letter he asked me to share my feelings about "God, Jesus Christ, and salvation." Having never fully developed an opinion on the matter, my response did not come easily. It required much study and personal exploration. In the days that followed, I was truly tested. Fear of losing my family if I embraced the gospel cumbered my every thought. The mental battle was almost too much.

I found myself pondering these very things one fall day as I stumbled through the center of campus on the way to class. Crowds of students rushed past me. They were walking together, speaking with one another, laughing. And me? Never before had I been encompassed by so many things and yet felt so alone. There was school, work, roommates, and the bustle of other students. It was a busyness I had never experienced before. Simply put, I was smothered, my spirit snuffed out. Looking heavenward, I sighed helplessly and with a release of that silent prayer a breeze swept by. It was neither a gust of wind nor a hurricane-strong blast, nothing miraculous, just a gentle breeze. All the same, it changed everything.

A calming chill pulsed through me as a flurry of auburn, burgundy and yellow-ochre leaves spiraled downward. Mimicking the leaves, I fell to the ground and buried myself within the tangled mass. Ignoring the puzzled looks of passers-by, I relished the moment. Enveloped in that blanket of leaves, I felt safe. The leaves, it seemed, came to life, and with their transformation, so did I.

The group dispersed, and I remained silently still as a single leaf migrated to my hand. It settled within the curved lining of my left palm. With the assistance of the wind it rocked back and forth in a teetering motion. The strokes felt good to weary skin. It was as though it understood my loneliness. It, of course, had just fallen from its own home and was now without the company of its loved ones, if it were possible that it could love.

I studied its small body and its complex vascular system. I saw within it, not a leaf but something entirely different. It was intangible and yet I wanted so badly to stretch that leaf to quilt size and wrap it around myself. It was impossible, I knew, but just the same, I imagined it hugging my body, lending the last of the life-blood coursing through its now giant veins. In that moment it became my savior and for the first time in my life the Atonement of our true Savior, Jesus Christ, became real. In my mind's eye I saw Him with outstretched arms. I no longer stood alone.

I finally knew what I needed and promised to take the steps necessary to make it all happen. Later, at home, I offered another prayer. I curled my hair. I dressed in my finest clothes. And I waited, staring out the front window, expectantly, for the local missionaries to come knocking at my door. They came!

For the better part of the next year, I met with the missionaries, discussing the truths of the gospel and addressing my many concerns and questions. Early on it became necessary to meet on campus, away from my home, as my roommate declared in no uncertain terms, "They can't come here." I spent the initial weeks of investigation avoiding her interrogations on the matter. These inevitable encounters soon turned to sincere questions, then into gospel-centered discussions. Still, the missionaries never again set foot in our home.

My dodging tactics weren't saved exclusively for my roommate. At times, I worked hard to evade the missionaries themselves. If I spied them outside our meeting place, I hid behind corners. If I thought they might call me, I let the phone ring. If they were even five minutes late for an appointment, I would walk straight past them telling them that, "if my time wasn't important to them, theirs wasn't important to me." They were late only once. This was a hard time, and, yet, I was noticeably changing.

I smiled more. Small obstacles in life became just that: small. They no longer had the power to weigh me down. I looked forward to meeting with the missionaries. We met outside in sunny locations. We met in quiet indoor spaces. I taught them to roller blade in church rooms generally reserved for important purposes. I came to fully accept their teachings. I began writing about these experiences to Mike and enjoyed our exchanges immensely. Our letters became more personal, and I quickly found myself falling, as they say, head over heels in love. I wanted this church in my life.

The answers I had yearned to know as a child were right before me.

I was torn. This might mean my family could abandon me. I couldn't risk that unless I knew for certain that I was making this decision for me and not just out of obligation or a fondness for Mike. An internal struggle grew. I obsessed over the matter. Uncharacteristically, my grades began to drop. Professors pulled me aside, concerned. Doubts entered my mind and my conviction waned. I didn't think I could possibly continue forward. I cancelled our meetings for a time.

Late on a summer night, during which the indoor thermometer read ninety-three degrees Fahrenheit, I lay sprawled, stomach side down, in a mass of tattered cotton sheets. My quilt and blanket clung precariously to the cliff side foot of the bed, having been violently kicked off with great irritation. Clammy hands acted as rotisserie equipment. Clenched to opposite poles of a pillow they periodically rotated in hopes of encountering cool pockets of fabric to press against sweltering skin. Sleep did not come easily. My body fought a constant battle to extinguish temporal flames. I tossed from side to side, clawed at soaked clothing and prayed for heat to meet its demise. I needed sleep to heroically march up to my bedside.

It wasn't just the temperature. I couldn't push aside the thought that I was making a terrible mistake. All I could think about was baptism. Somehow I managed to doze off, dreaming away a mental storm, only to be woken by a real batch of rain. I watched the water run down the window, felt of its coolness on the glass pane, and something switched inside. The rain, water, and baptism converged, and it all made perfect sense. Somehow, with the arrival of that outside storm, the one within me signaled its departure. Baptism seemed the obvious next step. I wanted it more than anything. I wanted to feel clean. I wanted past transgressions washed away.

I rushed outside. I felt excitement as water pressed against my skin. I stood in the downpour. I immersed myself in its moisture. My thoughts were cleansed. Every ounce of anger I once felt was released. I held out my arms, palms up, and reached for more drops, for the help of family and friends, and for the first time in my life, I reached out sincerely for the help of God. I prayed countless times that night and in return, my anger, sadness and confusion were washed away. It was the clearest moment I had ever experienced. Full of confidence, I worked my way back to the patio.

The downpour yielded. Delicate droplets pitter-pattered. I hugged a threadbare teddy bear, as childish as ever. I sought comfort from its matted fur and squeezed it for reassurance. I rested my nose upon its head and smelled for remnants of home. Sinking deeply into a padded chair, I watched cars whiz by and admired the beams of headlights reflect in the puddled rain. I smiled at the mist coming to life, emerging in a sense, from the warm, wet pavement. Although I was drenched, I sat in the dark with feet rested against the brick wall ahead of me and felt oddly warm. My soul had been nourished. I knew that things would be resolved. Exhausted, I slept soundly the remainder of that night.

I was at peace in the coming days. I made arrangements for baptism. I called my parents and informed them of my choice. Although surprised, they took it remarkably well. I wrote to Mike and shared the news. As you can imagine, he was elated. It felt wonderful to have finally attained the knowledge I had so desperately sought for as a child. Faith was no longer something to be feared but a gift well-earned and cherished.

The religious relics I remember as a child no longer decorate Mom's walls. I assume she has them, though, tucked away lovingly in secret places. I have held onto that first Bible given to me by my grandmother. I hold it close, and, although I study from a different printed version, that original Bible indeed planted seeds of faith. I sometimes still feel lonely and certainly experience earthly trials but face them willingly with hope and strength. I owe it all to a number of religious curiosities, a leaf spiraling in loneliness, a midnight rainstorm, and a treasured letter penned by Mike Schenk.

FIFTEEN

CONUNDRUM

Richard Timothy

Fun fact: having a favorite book doesn't need to have anything to do with the words inside.

Growing up, I hated reading, and yet, I loved books. The tactile feel of paper in my hands, the tiny crackle and thrum of a turning page, and the countless hours I'd spend making up stories thanks to imagination-inducing book covers. All of those things working in perfect harmony created my love affair with books . . . just as long as I didn't have to read what was inside.

A conundrum? Sure, but my dyslexia had a way of making me feel about reading the same way I felt about eating my vegetables—I'd usually end up crying whenever I had to try either. The one thing you need know about dyslexia—reading is hard.

When friends told me they read for fun the concept came across as something a Bond villain would concoct to wreak vengeance on humanity because of that one time a drunk frat kid shaved his cat. When they told me they just read their favorite book for the third time—what kind of sick freak—who does that? Not me, and I was certain I never would. Turns out, I didn't know my fourth-grade self as well as I thought. Over the years, I've encountered a handful of books I have come to call "favorite."

———

Fun fact: a book you hated reading can still become your favorite.

I encountered my first favorite book between fourth and fifth grade. I was forced to attend summer school, and the teacher, being a master of torture, had threatened that if I didn't read every night he'd fail me and I'd have to stay in 4th grade again instead of moving to 5th grade with my friends. He was an absolute monster.

When I explained these horrors to my mom, she confused me.

First she sided with me and gave me a hug, letting me know everything would be okay. Then she took the teachers side and suggested, "Let's go to the library and you can pick out your very own summer reading book. Whatever book you want."

I wasn't sold on the idea until she offered to make a batch of my favorite cookies when we got home. Twenty minutes later, we were off to the library.

When you hate reading, there are a number of factors to consider when selecting a summer reading book. First, font size. Bigger fonts = less words. Second, white space per page. I looked for excessive margins and small paragraphs. More white on the page = less words. Last, page count. If you get the first two working for you, you can easily find a 100 page book stretched out to around 200 pages. Visually impressive as long as no one looks at what's inside the book.

Based on this criteria, I found a few books to choose from. The second book in my stack was *The Box-Car Children* by Gertrude C. Warner. The cover did have a certain appeal. A group of kids living in a train boxcar. I could relate to wanting my own place. I was still sharing a room with my brother, Mike, and that son of a— kept stealing my Legos. Selecting this as my summer reading book happened quite naturally. Nature called while examining the book. On my way to the bathroom, I handed it to my mom. She checked out the book and was ready to go by the time I wandered out of the restroom.

My two-and-a-half-month relationship with this book was hell. If Beelzebub were reincarnated as a book, it would have been this one. Every night I fought with that story. On the worst nights I'd read only a sentence or two. On the best, I made it through a couple of pages. I dreaded bedtime because I knew reading would be required. I don't condone book burnings, but that damn paperback had me considering an exception.

Then, two weeks before school, the unexpected happened. The battle ended. I had kicked that book's ass, coming out as the victor. I had finished reading an entire book. A second later, I pronounced *The Box-Car Children* my first favorite book. Sure I hated reading it, but I loved that I'd read it.

My dyslexia always made me feel slower—dumber than the other kids in my class. But by reading a book cover to cover, I'd achieved something that the other kids did on a regular basis. For the first time since I'd realized I had a problem with reading, I felt normal. I was a regular kid, just like my classmates. I loved *The Box-Car Children* for giving me that feeling.

The other thing I'd learned: even though I didn't get along with reading, I could force myself to do it if I had to. Granted, it took a long-ass time, but it was possible.

———

Fun fact: you don't actually need to read a book for it to become your favorite.

Being thirteen taught me a very important lesson . . . deodorant is your friend. It also taught me it's not cool to have a book you read in fifth grade be your favorite. I had friends reading and talking about Asimov, and Heinlein, and the Dungeons & Dragons Forgotten Realms series, and I had nothing to offer. I did get good at asking questions about the characters on the covers. At least that way I could fake my way into reading related conversations with them.

I even considered adopting one of my assigned reading books as my new favorite. I could have picked *The Call of the Wild*, *The Pearl*, *The Outsiders*, or *To Kill a Mockingbird*, just to name a few. I had struggled through all of them thanks to my literature classes. The problem was I hated them all. They were all assignments. They had deadlines that kept me up until two or three o'clock in the morning reading because I read so slow. Then they were diagrammed and dissected, analyzed and discussed. They were all so much work that in the end I only saw them as collections of words that I hoped to never read again.

I considered explaining that I didn't have a favorite book for the simple reason there were no books out there good enough for me to call it a favorite. But I didn't have the personality skillset to pass myself off as a pretentious douche, so I bailed on that idea, too.

Turned out all I had to do was to stop looking for a favorite book. Instead, it found me.

The night *A Princess of Mars* by Edgar Rice Burroughs became my favorite book, I was sitting at the dinner table, alone, a little past 8 p.m. on a Thursday, eating a bowl of Rice Chex. Sure they get soggy faster than Corn Chex, but their crunch was far superior. I was half way through a bowl when Dave, my oldest brother, tapped me on the shoulder. As I looked up and beheld one of the most emotionally altering book covers a thirteen-year-old boy could fathom. The cover of *A Princess of Mars* painted by Michael Whelan.

Here's the thing about sci-fi and fantasy book covers from the '70s and '80s: so many were vastly superior to the lingerie section of the JC Penny catalogue, and with this cover . . . can I get a halleluiah. It consumed my thirteen-year-old mind and by the time I realized I was still holding a spoon, my Rice Chex were mush.

Dave sat down across from me and started telling me about Edgar Rice Burroughs. This was a new experience for me. Dave was in high school, instantly making him one of the coolest guys I knew. As the oldest, most of our communication consisted of him telling me to get up and manually change the channel on the TV during the commercials. So having him start telling me about an amazing book he'd just read was uncharted territory.

Over the next hour, he told me all about *John Carter*. Get this: he was an ex-soldier who gets teleported to Mars while escaping from

Apache Native Americans. And because of the gravity difference between Earth and Mars he was super strong and could jump around like a superhero. On Mars, which Martians called Bar-something, John meets *Tars Tarkas*, a giant green bug man warrior who becomes his best friend. He also gets his own Martian dog, *Woola*, who can move almost as fast as he can. And, last but not least, he finds a girlfriend, *Dejah Thoris*, who is a princess and doesn't like to wear clothes. As a puberty-plagued teenager, I couldn't image a more perfect story.

Still, it wasn't story that made *A Princess of Mars* my favorite book, it was the experience of having my brother share it with me. As the oldest brother, he won all the arguments and constantly picked on us. Oldest brother 101 really. But this was the first time I could recall him treating me like something more than a little brother. As he shared the story of John Carter, it felt like it did when I talked to my other friends about books. For that hour, for the first time in my life, my brother was a friend instead of a pestering big brother. I didn't realize that could happen until that night. *A Princess of Mars* gave me that experience, and for that it stayed my favorite book until the summer of 1993 . . . and I didn't have to read a single word.

Side note: It wasn't until twenty years later that I actually did read this book. Full disclosure: my brother's retelling was far superior to what I read. Sorry Edgar, Dave tells your story better.

———

Fun fact: turns out the end of the world can be the subject matter for the greatest book you'll ever read.

Once freed from the academic tedium call high school, I told higher education to suck it and dived headfirst into the job market. During that year, I purchased a few books, took comfort in not reading a single one all the way through, and filled up a notebook or two with really bad poetry.

During that summer, my best friend, Kyle, returned from his first year at college, and we spent the night drinking cheap beer and talking about the wonders of college. As he polished off his fourth can, realization filled his face.

"I have something for you," he said and reached into his backpack.

"I told you, I don't smoke that."

"Shut up." He laughed and started digging thought his pack. "Have you ever read Good Omens?"

"Never even heard of it."

His face lit up. "It's amazing. It's by Terry Pratchett and Neil Gaiman--he's the one that did the Sandman comics. It's about the end of the world, except so much more. It's fucking hysterical." He pulled out a disheveled paperback and handed it to me. "You have to read this. Trust me."

Skeptical I *had* to read anything, I thanked him for the gift and added, "I'll check it out as soon as I finish my current book."

There was no current book, but I'd discovered it was a great lie to use when to put off any and all reading suggestions indefinitely.

The problem was, apart from loving the band The Doors, I trusted Kyle's recommendations. He'd introduced me to most of my favorite bands, New Order, The Jesus and Mary Chain, and Bob Marley. He introduced me to *The Rocky Horror Picture Show*, the world of DC comics, and explained the importance of concert T-shirts, and the art of rolling up your pant legs. Then a few years later, the importance of not rolling up your pant legs. A very educational friend.

So, yeah, he could be trusted. Then again, it was a book. He'd also referred to it as "hysterical," which perplexed me. Hysterical and book were two words would never belong together.

After a week of mulling it over, the book got the better of me, and I finally took a peek. I expected to make it through the first five pages, the most I'd read of any book since graduation, and call it good. If asked how I liked it, I'd lie. I'd say it was an amazing read and never speak of it again.

Starting with the first page my face kept doing something if didn't do when I read. It kept smiling. Then came the line, "'A demon can get into real trouble, doing the right thing.' He nudged the angel."

I laughed—out loud. I stopped reading. Wait. What just happened? Had I really just laughed? No, not possible. There's no joy inside a book. I was certain of that. I was also certain I'd actually laughed out loud while reading. Probably a fluke. I started reading again to make sure.

Fifty pages later I peeked at the clock, it was 1:30 in the morning. I had to be up in two and a half hours for work. Stupid job—getting in the way of my reading. *Whoa, whoa, whoa. What the hell was happening to me?* I stopped reading mid-sentence and eyed the book's cover. The little minx. Nothing about this book matched what I knew about reading. It wasn't a punishment. When I got to a sentence I had to reread so it would make sense, it didn't matter. I was happy to do it. Even reading slow wasn't a hindrance. The story had me, and all I wanted was to find out what happened next.

I read every chance I got and finished the book three days later. I'd never read a book that quickly, and I haven't since. Afterwards, I kept thinking about why I'd responded that way to this book. If I had to put into one word what it was about *Good Omen* that made it my favorite book of all time, I'd have to say, "laughter."

This book revealed to me that a story could be more than fun, it could be funny. My own laughter while reading it showed me that a book didn't have to be a struggle; it could be a celebration instead. It showed me that humor and joy could be literary. I loved reading that book. And if that book was out there, maybe there were more that would make me feel the same.

I turned into a "born again" reader that summer, peddling literary joy to any willing to read the good book. I gifted at least ten copies of *Good Omens* that summer alone. Even today, I always have a spare copy in my house to pass along to the occasional visitor that has yet to read my favorite book.

I ended up going to college with a focus on art, but after a few years I realized that painting never made me feel the way reading *Good Omens* did. I started writing more and painting less. Eventually,

I shifted my focus and graduated with a degree in English. A degree I am challenged by and grateful for every day.

My personal experience with reading *Good Omens*, is a constant reminder for why I want to share humor in my writing. It's the book that changed my life, and for that it will always be my favorite.

SIXTEEN

A VERY FINE STEW

Bryan Young

The sheriff staggered from his front door, probably still drunk. His sword belt wasn't even around his waist; he'd thrown it over one shoulder and let his sword dangle uselessly at his side. Every few feet he'd stagger and the tip would dig into the ground before he got upright again.

He pounded on the door of the tavern that had been closed for an hour. The last candles had been snuffed and the barkeep had gone to bed. The last thing she'd probably wanted to deal with was a drunk. Doubly so for a drunk man of the law with a chip on his shoulder.

"Evlyn," he shouted. "Open up, Evlyn! We want a drink."

But Evlyn was sleeping.

The whole town was sleeping.

That didn't matter to the sheriff.

Nothing did.

"Evlyn!"

The sound of his fist smashing against the heavy oak door carried into the night of the town. A cricket chirped until a horse neighed in the stables.

When Evlyn never came, he lowered the top of his trousers and pissed all over the door. And his boots. His hands, too.

When he finished up, he wiped his hands on his shirt and kept walking along as though he'd forgotten he was thirsty in the first place.

The jailhouse wasn't far.

He staggered there to sleep it off on the cot in his office. Just another typical night.

The cock crowed and the sun rose that morning. The night had remained quiet and the sheriff was still asleep.

Evlyn knew that when the sheriff woke, there would be hell to pay. Not for any reason in particular, but when he had a headache he made sure everyone else had a headache, too.

It was the first of the month and he'd begin his rounds by collecting coppers for the crown. It wouldn't have been so bad if he wasn't so consistently abrasive about it. It made one wish the stories of the Hood were real and she'd come and take care of the sheriff and make sure he wouldn't harass anyone ever again. And maybe get those coppers back to someone who could use them.

Especially since it seemed like the sheriff always had nicer finery every Tax Day and the "first of the month" seemed to happen every couple of weeks instead of monthly. Folks had taken to saving everything just in case the sheriff came by unexpectedly.

There was no bit of awfulness he wouldn't perpetrate. He'd smack the children of the village around. He'd grope at the women in the tavern. Or the men in the church. It didn't really matter. Unfortunately for everyone, he was the law in town until the judge arrived to conduct his trials. He could do what he liked in the meantime. There was no crossing him if you didn't want him to make your life a nightmare.

He was the definition of a bully.

"I'm going to kill him," Evlyn said, looking down at the sheriff through the crude glass window on the second floor of her tavern.

There was no hesitation in her voice. No regret. The only note in the melodious song of her voice was resolve.

"Shh," Tilly said back to her. "They'll hear."

"Hear how?"

"Magic," Tilly said matter-of-factly in a low tone.

"He's got no magic," Evlyn said. "He's a two-bit thief, and a bully, and that's it. If he had magic he'd be working for the crown at the tower. Not here, harassing us at all hours."

"But what of the magistrate?"

"The judge don't have magic neither," Evlyn said. "He'd be working at the tower, too. You don't get to be a judge or a sheriff if you've got magic."

"I haven't made it as far as I have without being suspicious of what could be done to me with a little bit of magic," Tilly said.

"Tilly, you're the barkeep in my tavern, which you don't own. How far've you really come?"

"My parents raised goats and now I work in a proper building."

"Fair enough, I suppose." Evlyn shrugged and stared out the window, watching the sheriff carry on his rounds. He'd be at the tavern soon enough. She didn't want to get into it again with Tilly about superstition. It was the Coroner Warlocks she'd need to worry about. They'd be the ones with the magic. She'd have to be careful to outwit them if she was going to go through with it.

Hiding the evidence would be the hardest part.

Killing was easy.

The real worry was what to do with the body once the job was done.

And how to make sure no one was around to witness it.

No one would miss him; that part would be easy enough.

No one but the crown, anyway. They'd have to send another sheriff. Their only hope would be that they'd get assigned a sheriff that was less corrupt. And if he wasn't, Evlyn supposed she would take care of them, too.

"Ma'am?" Tilly said.

"Huh?" Evlyn snapped out of it. "What was that?"

"I said, 'Do you want me to bring up another cask of the cider?'"

"Yes, Tilly. That'll be fine. Bring up a second barrel of mead, too." She looked back down at the sheriff. "I think we're going to need it."

———

The Ugly Dove teemed with life.

Everyone was there in the evenings and that's just how Evlyn liked it.

Drifters coming through town, passing on their way to the capital, were always a good portion of the business. The other bit was the regular crowd. The townsfolk were always as reliable a source of business as the travelers. They'd all stay all night if they could. If Evlyn let them.

But Evlyn needed time to herself. So, she kept the tavern closed from the second chimes after midnight until the second chimes after noon. It just made things bearable for her.

The hardest her life got was around midnight at the Ugly Dove until closing. When she started cutting people off of the booze, they could get a little unruly. No one wanted to end their good time, but neither did anyone want to get in the way of Evlyn's wishes.

Well, that wasn't exactly the truth. The *actual* hardest was midnight to closing at the Ugly Dove when the sheriff needed to leave.

He'd start fights and argue. There were a few times where closing the bar with him, drunk off his ass, could be downright terrifying. Part of it was because she could never guess how he was going to react. If he reacted poorly, would he even remember the next day when he came to?

There were days where the memory of getting removed from the tavern had slipped him by in a blackout of drink. There were other days where he remembered and came back at opening to make Evlyn's life hell. "It's the first of the month," he'd say, sidling up to the back door with a sneer on his face and an extended palm.

It was a very oblique way to ask for a bribe, and Evlyn always paid.

She'd hear stories from all the townsfolk who had to endure the same thing. Any infraction was met with "the first of the month."

Evlyn wondered what he did with all the money since, aside from the finery he wore and promptly soiled, there was nothing of wealth that marked him. Did he drink it all? He spent a lot at the Ugly Dove, but that always got paid back in the form of "taxes."

She wondered if he was a gambler.

Or if he hired mercenaries to do dark work elsewhere.

That theory didn't make sense because he always seemed to do just fine in sowing his own terror across the town.

Evlyn worried that he sent the money he skimmed off to some aged relative that couldn't fend for themselves.

"Another ale!" The sheriff's voice and the *thunk* of his tankard against the bar snapped Evlyn back from her daydream. She was helping Tilly tend the bar and keep the fires stoked. She'd need to bring on more help if the bar stayed as busy as it had been.

Evlyn knew it was coming time to cut everyone off and send them on their way, but she obliged the sheriff. "Here you are, Sheriff," she said, taking his cup and filling it once more at the cask.

"That's right," he muttered to no one in particular.

She handed him his ale and he buried his face in it. When he pulled the glass from his mouth, his mustache was soaked with froth and drink dribbled down the sides of his beard.

"I want another one, too, Evlyn," Samael said from his perch two stools from the sheriff.

No one sat *next* to the sheriff. That was inviting trouble.

"I want another, too," Theresa said with a giddiness in her voice that told Evlyn she'd need to be cut off before she started putting all the ale she'd drank back onto the bar. She was notorious for that.

But Evlyn arched an eyebrow and aimed it Samael and Theresa. "It's about closing time. This one's just for the sheriff."

The sheriff, slurring his words, growled at them. "Yeah… Hear that? It's just for me."

"Finish your beers and out before the chimes," Evlyn told them.

The sheriff took another long draught of his new beer and

when he finished, shouted, "Another," as he tossed the tankard across the bar. "I'm not leaving till I've had my fill."

He'd aimed his cup at the bottles of mulled wine Evlyn had kept back there, but his throw was impotent and his cup hit the back shelf, fell on the floor, and rolled onto Tilly's feet.

"Hells of fire," she muttered. She stopped herself from saying more when she realized who had thrown the cup.

Evlyn leaned over to Tilly and put a hand on her shoulder. Then, Evlyn whispered to her. "It's fine, Tilly. I've got this. Help me clear the bar and I'll take care of the sheriff on my own. I think it's going to be a rough one."

Tilly nodded and went about the tavern, picking up empty tankards and collecting the money from the assembled crowd before sending them on their way.

The sheriff dug the tip of his dagger into the wood of the bar counter. "Another one," he said in a dark, low voice.

"Coming right up, Sheriff," Evlyn said.

Picking up his tankard from the floor, she filled it. There was no use in dirtying a clean one for him. He wouldn't notice the difference. As she put the ale in front of him, she hoped he didn't drain it as quickly as the last time. She still had plenty of work to do and didn't want to stand over him any longer.

It was always best to be just out of arm's reach where the sheriff was concerned.

Evlyn and Tilly managed to shoo everyone out just after the second bell after midnight. Once the tables had been polished and the money locked away, Evlyn shooed Tilly out the door, too.

But Tilly didn't want to go. "You can't just stay here alone with him," she whispered harshly as Evlyn tried to close the door on her.

The sheriff was hunched over at the bar. Whether he noticed that the place had emptied, Evlyn couldn't say. He just nursed his ale, bleary-eyed.

"It's fine," Evlyn said. "It's all fine."

Tilly's skeptical eyes locked with Evlyn's, but Evlyn wouldn't hear any more about it. Just as Tilly took in a breath to protest further, Evlyn shut the door on her. Then, before she could push back on it, Evlyn dropped the sturdy oaken crossbar into place.

Then she smiled.

————

When Judge Fernandez arrived in the small town, the first thing he'd heard were whispers. Whispers about a great many things, but chief among them was the disappearance of the sheriff. He'd been gone for three days and had vanished without a trace.

This was mildly troubling to the judge.

He had arrived in town to collect the crown's coin for the taxes and to dispense any delayed justice that might be had. But with no sheriff in town, it made things difficult. He didn't even know where to begin his normal work. It would all have to wait until he got to the bottom of the sheriff's disappearance.

Naturally, the good judge began at the sheriff's home.

There, he found no traces that anyone had been living there for at least a few days. The pisspots were full of old, rancid waste, the shelves were full of cheese and bread that had molded over.

Something must have happened, because the sheriff had been a paunchy fellow, at least as far as the judge could remember from his last visit to town, and wouldn't let food go to spoil. It wasn't like him.

The judge was dismayed to find no sign of a strongbox full of the collected taxes, either. But there was probably a much more likely chance of finding it at the jailhouse where the sheriff's office was located. It made sense that it could be kept there.

But when the judge searched the jailhouse, the only thing he found were the telltale signs of a slob.

Quickly, he decided he'd need to question the townsfolk if he was going to get to the bottom of this mystery and collect the taxes on behalf of the Queen

Sheriffs didn't just disappear overnight.

Naturally, the next place the judge went was the tavern. Taverns were hubs of information and everyone was always a little looser of tongue with a few stiff ales in them.

As evening drew on, the judge hitched his horse to the posts outside and entered. The Ugly Dove teemed with life. It was more than life, though. It was merriment. It seemed odd that people would be in such cheer when the sheriff of their town, the representative of the Crown, was missing under such mysterious circumstances.

There were three empty chairs at the bar and the judge aimed straight for the middle one. He smoothed his hands over the bar and wondered what sort of establishment let their place fall into such disrepair. Where the bar should have been well worn and polished, there were blemishes and stabs in the wood.

The tavern keeper met him with a broad smile and she asked, "What can I fix for you today, Your Honor?"

"A spot of food," he said, dropping a shiny coin on the battered bar. "And an ale, if you please."

The woman clapped her hands together and rubbed them. "I've just the thing for you."

She scooped the coin up, placed it in the pocket in her smock, and went about her work, preparing a helping of lunch for him. The judge was left to brood in his thoughts in the din of the room.

Where would the sheriff have gone?

Why would he have left with no notice?

It hadn't appeared as though anything had been taken, aside from the lockbox.

And that's when wheels began to turn in the judge's mind.

The woman behind the bar arrived with a wooden bowl full of meat stew that smelled heavenly, as well as a chunk of hot bread and a nice plate of cheese. Then, she turned to fill the ale.

The judge leaned over the stew and took the scent in. He could make out the strong smell of game, but it was balanced neatly with vegetables, the onions and carrots, as well as strong, leafy herbs he couldn't quite identify. The sauce was thick, and he couldn't wait to dig in.

The tavern keeper slid the ale toward him across the bar and she stood there with an expectant smile. "Well, how is it?"

Obliging her, the judge tore a hunk from the bread and dipped it into the steaming stew. Then he blew on it before taking a meaty bite. The flavor hit him at once. The gaminess of the meat was balanced perfectly against the other ingredients and his mouth watered for more. He nodded his approval and spoke with a mouth half full. "It's very good."

"Good. It's a new recipe I've worked up. I'm not sure how long I'll be able to keep it up, but I'm glad you got to try it while it lasted."

"Me as well," he said, pinching a chunk of the meat with a piece of the bread and devouring it.

"Is there anything else I can help you with, Your Honor?" she asked.

"Well," he swallowed down the rest of his bite, "I have a few questions, if you don't mind."

She blushed and the judge wondered if she was concerned he was going to ask something untoward. "No, no, nothing like that. It's about the sheriff."

"Oh, the sheriff. Good riddance, I say."

"I take it he wasn't well-liked in town, then?"

"Well, to tell the truth Your Honor, he wasn't. I mean, he'd go around groping everyone. He'd smack the children around. He wouldn't pay his debts. He once cornered my barmaid and practically put the demon fear in her. And that's just the polite list of things to say about him. Since he split town, it's been quiet and peaceful around here. It's like we've got our town back again."

"Is that it then? You think he just up and left town?"

"I mean, what else is there? You think somebody murdered him?"

The judge thought for a moment and then took another bite of the stew. He tried to imagine the most gruesome fate he could for a sheriff despised by their town and didn't want to offend the poor woman with those thoughts, so he kept them to himself. He swallowed. "Well, when people are desperate, anything can happen."

"I suppose," she said. "The thing that matters most to me is the safety of everyone. It's a hard thing to imagine a place that's safer when the sheriff is gone, but that just goes to show how bad he was."

The judge tilted his head. What she was saying bordered on sedition. The sheriff, bad as he might have been, was a duly appointed representative of the crown. "Surely, you don't question the crown's judgement in appointing a sheriff?"

"No, Your Honor. I would never. I don't think they knew what sort he'd be when he got here."

He washed the cheese down with the ale then went back to the bowl of stew. He couldn't stay away from it.

"I must say, this really is the best stew I've had in months."

The tavern keeper bowed her head to him and curtsied a bit. "Why, thank you, Your Honor."

"You really will have to put down the recipe so that I can give it to my wife."

"Oh, she wouldn't want this recipe."

"But I think she'd love it. It's not magic is it?" he said, instantly suspicious.

"No, no sir; no magic."

The tavern keeper winked and leaned in to whisper. "The secret is brining the meat in alcohol."

"I see."

"No magic at all. Tell you what, I'll put down what I can and you stop in on your way out of town before you go. I'll make sure you have a recipe and another full helping before you're gone."

"Oh, I would love that. Many thanks."

"It's my pleasure, Your Honor. Now, did you have any other questions for me before I tend to the others?" She waved her rag around, indicating the rest of the tavern.

"No," the judge said, sopping up the last bit of stew with his bread and taking a last heaping bite. "I think what's happened is apparent."

"And for the better if you ask me."

"Indeed," the sheriff said. "I'll be away tomorrow. We'll send out posters and offer a reward for the capture of the sheriff. No one steals from the crown and gets away with it. And when we find him, we'll know exactly what happened, dead *or* alive."

The tavern keeper took the bowl from him and stared into the dirtied dish. "I've got a sneaking feeling we won't be seeing the likes of him again."

"All the same." The judge polished off his ale and dropped the empty tankard on the bar as well.

He wiped his mouth with his sleeve, disappointed with the sheriff. But, like the tavern keeper said, everyone did seem happy. The spirits in the room were high, higher than he'd seen in any town he'd visited so far. There was cheer and laughter echoing from one side of the tavern to the other.

And that made him smile.

As he wondered how quickly he could circulate the posters, he belched loudly, bringing all the rich flavor back onto his breath.

It really was a very fine stew.

SEVENTEEN

THE LODGE

Johnny Worthen

"The trappers had built their cabin over an old Indian camp."

"You're going there? Seriously?"

"It's a good story."

"Kyle, this is the kind of shit that happens with humanities majors. In STEM we don't make shit up."

"I didn't make it up. I'm telling you what the professor told me."

"But with embellishments?"

"Of course. I'm a writer, baby."

"And it was Rouke who told you this?"

"The NIMBYs asked him to do a historical survey."

"So he's on the other side?"

Kyle nodded. "He didn't get it. He practically busted a gut to tell me, even after I told him he was working against my dad."

"Another example of flutter-brained arts majors."

"Humanities—history professor, with a doctorate."

"That's what I said."

"Do you want to hear the story or don't you?"

"Fine fine." Brad fanned a paper plate over the budding fire. Smoldering newspaper flared in a flameless orange glow then caught and spread to the fire-starting sticks they'd brought with them.

"Make sure the flue is open," said Kyle.

"It is."

"Then why is the room filling with smoke?"

Brad gave him a look and then peeked up the chimney. He reluctantly reached inside and pushed the lever. The flannel on his sleeve flared and balled as the hot smoke was sucked out and into the cold mountain air and the sticks glowed blue with chemical fuel and new air.

"Don't put the big logs on until the medium—"

"Tell your damn story," Brad said.

"Maybe I should save it for the girls," said Kyle.

"You do have more than one story, right?"

"Har har."

Brad fiddled with the grate, and jabbed a poker into the fire to shift things around. "An old Indian burial ground," he said. "Got it. Go on."

"Not a burial ground, a campsite."

"Ooooo, a campsite? That is so much scarier."

Kyle wiped meat off the end of his knife and waved the blade at his friend like an accusing finger. "Enough of your sass, young man."

Brad gave him the finger and they both laughed.

Outside, through the window over the sink, Kyle saw the sky was ashen slate and the little light that found its way through the cabin windows was low and murky. The snow cover outside, though icy and old, had not light enough to sparkle the frost. A storm was coming. Ski reports offered a thirty percent chance of flurries by the late afternoon to finalize the cloud cover they'd had all day.

It would be great cuddling weather, and Kyle chopped and cooked with warm expectations of holing up for a few days with his best friend and their best girls. Roughing it in luxury. Season passes and just a hill between them and a black diamond mogul run. He looked forward to the shared solitude and was glad that his father had been unsuccessful turning the cheaply bought land into over-priced condos.

Ski-in condos had been the plan when the resort announced new boundaries. Kyle's father, however, had been unable to get past the planning commission. He needed permits for a road, sewer and water. And now there were the neighbors, the NIMBYs - Not In My Back Yard - complainers who promised to battle him until the next century—and this one had just begun. In the meantime, more as proof of concept than long term investment, Kyle's dad had built this great, underutilized ski retreat. Kyle had every belief that he'd inherit the zoning fight along with this lodge when his father died. He was an only child.

"It's a natural campsite," Kyle went on. He pushed the meat and carrots into the pot, put it in the sink and pumped water up from the spigot.

"And so convenient," Brad said, his sarcastic gaze aimed squarely at the antique water pump.

"It is, actually. Dumbass," said Kyle. "It's flat. There's a spring. Lots of sheltering trees."

"Great powder."

"The trappers didn't have the same appreciation for that that we do. I can't speak to the Indians."

"It's choice."

"There is something about this place," he said.

"I'll stop dissing it."

"You can put on a big log now," Kyle said.

"I know how to build a fire."

"Tell that to the flue."

Kyle turned the stove on and a blue propane flame leaped up to meet the heavy pot. The smooth, spicy smell of pepper and chives, chicken and broth, made Kyle's stomach gurgle. Though power came from generators, heat from a fireplace and two wood stoves, and water from the antique pump, the cabin was otherwise a modern house. It had a full kitchen, three comfortable bedrooms, two bathrooms, and art on the walls—water colors of elk and cowboys, Indian women smoking meat, a trapper with a mule. One was of a clown with big eyes painted on black velvet. Supposedly that one was valuable.

The wind blew a gust and the door rumbled pulling Kyle's attention to the big mudroom where he could see their skis set against the wall, their coats hanging on hooks, but not the entrance.

"You closed the door right?" asked Kyle.

"Do you see a snow drift in here?"

"No."

"Then I damn well closed it, didn't I?"

Kyle stirred the pot, added a soup mix for flavor, a touch of salt. "The girls are what? An hour away?"

"Closer to two, I'd bet. They'll wait to be sure the house is good and warm before they even put on their parkas this time. We won't see them before four."

It took about an hour to get the house awake and habitable after sitting empty for a month. The last time they'd come, the girls were wet from a drizzly storm, cold from falling in the deep snow, short-tempered and hungry. When they finally got inside, they complained and sulked together until the fire was lit, not taking off their coats until the cabin was a sauna and they'd each had a bowl of soup and two margaritas. This time the boys arrived early to get the place cozy and warm for a good long weekend break between semesters.

"Trappers," said Brad. "Trappers—remember? Man, even in your bullshit stories, you wander. Your mind ain't right."

"There were two of them—the trappers. French. Axel Fournier and Theodore Durand."

"You know the names?"

"It made the papers."

"What did?"

"I'll get there."

"Then do." Brad closed the fire grate and flopped on the couch. He unzipped his Tau Sigma Phi jacket and put his feet up on the coffee table.

Kyle remembered Professor Rouke's excitement when he'd told him. He'd been full of dates and references, myths and folktales.

Kyle decided he would add a bit of drama, use his humanities chops, theme, parallel, and malaise. If it played well on Brad, he'd tell it to the girls even better.

"It was toward the end of the fur trade," Kyle said stirring. "The two men had trapped together for years. They were the best of friends." Rouke hadn't told him that, but it felt right and so he went with it. "They'd trapped across three states and ended up here in the Wasatch Mountains chasing the last few beavers in the area before civilization came in and the hat fad went out."

"My friend the author," said Brad.

"Humanities, baby. Where the mind is free."

"Where the mind is warped," said Brad. "Come on. Crack a beer, Shakespeare. Sit down. We got time."

Kyle adjusted the stove and snapped a couple of cans from the case before sitting down across from his friend. The fire was bright and warm, already heating the room to a tolerable level, and like his friend, Kyle unzipped his jacket and relaxed.

"So they were best friends," said Brad. "Known each other since grade school? Lived on the same street growing up? Roommates in college?"

"The were from Quebec," said Kyle, unfazed. "There are mentions of them both in the records of the Rendezvous."

"The big drunk mountain man party?"

"Yeah."

"Cheers!" Brad tilted back his beer with a grin.

"Bridger also recorded—"

"From Quebec. Hunted three states. Came to Utah. Stay on target, Red One."

"You're fun to talk to."

"Just keeping your wandering mind on course, old buddy."

"Axel Fournier scouted this place and built a rough cabin, staying a year alone in it while Durand took their furs to St. Louis. They met up in late summer at Fort Bridger."

"Durand is Teddy?"

"Theodore, yeah."

"And the year was?"

"I don't remember."

"Rouke would be disappointed."

"I know, right?" said Kyle. "I can't believe I don't remember that kind of detail when no one was interrupting him."

"Fine fine. Go on."

Kyle smirked and sipped his beer, it was cold and icy, but warmed him inside. The house was cozy and intimate. The fire crackled and cast orange tinged shadows over the carpeted floor. While the food cooked and the cabin warmed, Kyle told his story.

———

The trappers should have had good time to make it to their winter cabin. The hard part, the long journey was behind them—Durand's trek from St. Louis across great plains and sullen rivers, but early snow found them still packing in Fort Bridger, Wyoming.

It was a quick squall, blew in and out, and left only a few inches of snow, but it promised a long and hard winter. The men set out at once.

Carrying all they had on their backs or pulling it in wide travois, they set left the fort aiming west and south over Indian roads and deer trails. Soon the Wyoming plains turned to low hills and then high peaks. Following a river gorge, they came out into a wide empty valley.

"Our place is up there around that second canyon," said Fournier.

"That's the Great Salt Lake there?" asked Durand pointing to the water in the far distance.

"It is," said Fournier. "It's a poisoned hole. There's a better lake in the south, fresh water there, but the area looks like to have been trapped out. And there are Indians."

"And the place you found is good?"

"It is a great place to overwinter," Fournier said. "High and sheltered. There's water. The Indians won't bother us."

"Why's that?"

"Long story."

"Can't wait to hear it."

At the mouth of their canyon, the snow began. It took them a day and half to reach the shelter. The slope was mild but made hard by the deepening snow. When they broke out of the tree line Fournier was pleased at how picturesque and pleasant the little meadow was, and their cabin nestled within it. Tire and sore, sleep deprived, the men threw themselves onto the frozen dirt floor and rested the moment they were inside.

Fournier woke before his friend and set the cabin right. He stored their supplies and rolled out buffalo furs for bedding over the floor. He set a pot of meal to boil and another for coffee while Durand slept.

All the while it snowed outside.

Durand woke to the smell of hot food and coffee and smiled with relief and gratitude.

"I thought I was dreaming that," he said. He looked around the space, peering into the corners and low ceiling by the light of the fire and a single lamp. "Is it night?"

"I think so, but I can't be sure," said Fournier. "We're already snowed in."

"What?"

Fournier went to the rough door and pulled it open to show a blocking wall of white beyond. "We've been here a day and it hasn't stopped for a moment. It could still be snowing."

Durand nodded his head and grimacing, having scalded his mouth on a cup of boiling coffee.

They'd expected this. This is how one wintered in the high mountains. They made to be bears, holed up and fed, waiting for conditions to change, for spring, for the sun to come and the snow to go. This year it had come earlier than expected, but they were ready for that, safe in their hole.

The men stretched out on the furs and ate stew in a silence that bespoke their long friendship and deep understanding. Fournier was pleased when Durand produced a new deck of cards and they had their first game of the season.

They did not know how long the storm lasted or the next or the next, nor how deep the snow had become. "Less than twelve feet," was what Fournier said because that was the height of their chimney. "Then again, it could be more and the heat has made a tunnel."

Durand thought that was unlikely. "If it's much taller, it'll cave in eventually and then we'd know it."

That first week, they dug a tunnel from the doorway to the woodshed and kept the piles high in the cabin, making it their daily routine more as a way to keep time than by any immediate necessity.

They played cards, rationed their coffee, and waited.

Weeks went by. Months.

They spent most days in silence, comfortable and enduring. They'd known each other since childhood and had nothing new to discuss and were comfortable in it, like the little cabin itself, insulated and safe.

It was some time before Durand finally asked Fournier about the Indians and the tale he promised on the trail.

Axel was shocked to remember he hadn't told his friend the story. "Oh, it is a good yarn," he said.

"Do tell. I'll make time. Message the baron, I will be busy this afternoon."

Fournier threw a log in the fire, preparing to speak more in the next hour than he had all month.

"The story as I understood it was about two friends who stayed here. In this very spot. In this very meadow."

Durand lay back contentedly. Fournier saw the excitement in his face. A new yarn was a thing to rejoice. He cleared his throat and embellished.

"They were best friends and had been warned of this place."

"Oh?" said Durand.

"Yes, the older peoples had warned them."

"What's wrong with here?"

"I'll get there, Theodore," said Fournier. "Sit back and listen."

"Very well, very well."

"So even before the Indians there was——"

"Is the door closed?" asked Durand.

Axel turned and felt the draft. How air could move so fast through the tunnel to shake the door, he was uncertain. He could see though that the door was closed. He pushed a shirt into the gap at the bottom to stop the breeze and returned.

"Who told you this?" said Durand.

"An Indian woman—a shaman," Fournier hoped that his friend wouldn't recognize the obvious lie there. Utes don't have female shamans.

"Go on."

"So the Indian braves knew the history, knew the curse of the place."

"A curse now?"

"Yes, why not?"

"You read too much, Axel," said Durand.

Fournier ignored the comment. He was never sure if he was being teased or complimented. Theodore often chided him for wasting his mind on fantasy and imagination, but then again, he never complained when Axel found a new novel and read it to him at night after a long day's work pulling glorified rats from steel traps in icy rivers.

"So the braves…" coaxed Durand.

"They knew the stories, but the place was so amicable that they chose to build a hunting lodge here. There was much game nearby. Deer, elk. Beaver. They made a smoking rack and a lean-to and planned to spend a week or so before heading back to their village, big men for all the meat."

"Let me guess," said Durand. "It started snowing?"

"Yes. Exactly."

"So goes the legend."

Fournier winked at his friend. "They holed up in the lean-to but the snow was so heavy they soon found themselves trapped and running low on food."

Fournier saw his friend's eyes flash over to their food supply and return to him contentedly. Fournier glanced too and counted three full crates of provisions. Coffee, sugar, meal. Smoked meat. A year's worth.

Getting back in the mood, he said. "It came up on them suddenly."

"What did?"

"The woman wouldn't say. When she came to the name, she fell silent, the gap being the name. I didn't know if she meant a curse, or a devil, or a madness." He paused for effect, the fire crackled and the pot steamed.

"The one leapt upon his friend," he said. "He drove his flint knife into his throat and ripped it open. A stare of horror and surprise met the attack as the Indian drank the gushing blood like it was a desert spring and he'd been wandering the sands thirsty for weeks."

Durand stared at him, captivated.

Fournier pulled his knife off his belt for effect.

"While his friend still lived, sucking breaths—his last ones, gurgling and disbelieving, the killer butchered him into strips of meat."

Fournier paused for effect holding the knife over his head dramatically.

"When he got to the liver he took a big bite out of it, savoring the flavor—food to a starving man. He slurped and sucked and moaned in delight. He stuck the leftover liver on a spit and cooked it in the fire while he prepared the rest of the meat for the smokehouse."

Fournier's eyes unfocussed and he felt ill.

The draft was back and he looked to see if perhaps his friend had left to relieve himself, or more hopefully, vomit for the terror of the story. He thought it'd told it well.

The door was shut.

Turning back to Durand, he saw the mess. Durand was cut to pieces. A piece of meat sizzled in the fire place, the room smelled of wet metal and roasting game.

He had no recollection of what he had done, but looking at his hands he saw his own bloody knife. Licking his lips, he tasted thick congealing rust. Sucking his teeth, he found shreds of raw meat, gamey, spongy, and fresh.

"The old trapper, Fournier, screamed. It was all he could do. Scream. He screamed and screamed. For days they say he screamed, until a passing—"

A gust of wind shook Kyle out of the tale and he turned to looked down the hall. Melissa and Anne stood in the doorway, their pink and purple parkas wet with new melting snow.

"Thanks for getting the place ready for us," Melissa said. "Feels warm. Smells good."

"Is that barbecue?" asked Anne. "I thought we were having stew."

"What's on your—"

They paused a step farther in. Their eyes grew big. They stared and stumbled.

Slowly, Kyle turned toward the fire, to where Brad had been. The blood was black in the carpet, pooled on the couch. Meat— clean cut pink strips of it, lay on coffee table, ready for the smoke house and a half-eaten liver sizzled seductively in the fireplace.

EIGHTEEN

DAMN THE UNICORNS

Jef Huntsman

Damn the unicorns.
Screw the whales.
I'm cruising 40 knots
with billowed sail.

Good riddance to the sea turtle
and the coral reef that's bare.
Vessels a rolling,
what the hell do I care?

Breathe in the fumes.
Love sucking tainted CO_2.
My wake's deep and sure,
all else can get screwed.

Dig those wells.
Frack the earth.
Baby has six arms.
It's only a birth.

Bicycle riders,
And energy saving queens.
Keep to your place
in your pre-washed jeans.

The motors are racing.
We're heading with flair.
Can't stop and think,
or we'll never get there.

NINETEEN

ME IN THE CITY OF ROCKS

Virginia Babcock

I have always wondered why my great-great-grandpa left Utah for California more than one hundred and fifty years ago. When I found great-great-grandma's journal in my father's papers I learned the answer and found the rest of the story.

I traveled to the middle of nowhere in southern Idaho to the City of Rocks to better understand the answer. I had my own troubles on this journey, but none came close to what my great-great-grandparents had endured.

On that day, I gratefully made it the last fifty feet to my Jeep parked on the side of the freeway. I had taken a three mile journey to and back from a tiny gas station where I paid twenty dollars for a used two-gallon gas tank and its two gallons of gas. I poured it into my tiny gas tank knowing that in about ten minutes I'd get ten dollars back for the can when I returned to the station and filled the tank. That gas station was the only one within thirty miles and the only one between me and the City of Rocks.

Thankfully, the engine started. As I pulled onto the deserted highway I recalled some of great-great-grandmother's words.

Harold survived the night. My actions to cut his leg and suck out the venom must have helped. His leg is awful to behold. The skin is taut and purple with swelling around the wound. But it bleeds clear with no puss. He shudders and cries hoarsely for water, but the burden of our child keeps me from venturing to the rocky creek bed in this dark night. I fell this morning when I brought the last batch of water, and though I do not bleed, the babe seems listless. I will spend the remains of this night near my shivering husband as I pray that both he and our babe survive until morn. I pray that whatever happens I can hitch the mules to our wagon and move on soon.

I'd chosen to enter the City of Rocks Reserve from the Malta side near Albion. Coincidentally, Grandma had lived in Albion for a time and driving this tiny but paved country road reminded me of her. She told me of her grandmother who'd lost so much along this road, and had also told me I looked like great-great-grandma. It was the hair and eyes. Our family was mostly dark-haired and dark-eyed, but now and then we'd spawn a red-headed, blue-eyed relation. I was the latest recessive in the bunch.

Memorial Day seemed like a fitting time to take a trip to reminisce on dead family members; I also needed to get away. I'd hoped for sunshine, blue skies, and the green grass of early summer. Looking through the windshield, I saw gray skies rolling with dark clouds. The storm had built up in intensity since dawn. I'd been lucky to make it back to the Jeep before the rain started. Fat drops bombarded my vehicle as I bounced it along the bumpy road.

The City of Rocks Visitors Center parking lot was pretty full. The rain had forced some into the commercialized house to shop and chat with the National Park Service Rangers. I elbowed my way through what used to be an old lady's parlor to reach the Rangers' desk to pay my entrance fee. A quick pit stop to what used to be the old lady's restroom, and I was grateful to be back out in the rain.

Rain is actually my kind of weather. Living in the high deserts of the Intermountain West has taught me to praise the rain when it falls. Thunder rumbled overhead, and I spared a moment to meditate on the possibility of lightning striking me while scrambling over tall granite boulders and outcrops. I resolved to guide myself in the park trusting what others were doing, though I knew it would be foolish to scramble over large rocks in a thunderstorm. I'd be the highest point and surely be inviting trouble.

The pavement ended, and I drove on a well-maintained dirt road. The park map of the area showed me how well the road followed the old California Trail the pioneers had followed. A few miles out of the park, I stopped. An old homestead caught my eye. Its farmhouse stood in a narrow valley just off the road near the creek that ran along the trail. The house looked decrepit, but the barns and outbuildings appeared well-kept. I glanced westward and saw a newer home situated a bit further on and suspected a later generation had built a new, bigger house on the family farm. The proximity to the City of Rocks valley and the creek made me think of the next passage from great-great-grandma's diary.

Harold is better today physically. In his heart, things are worse. He stares at Mr. Brighton with hatred in his eyes. I fear he's imagining Mr. Brighton has taken some improper action toward me. I've explained he's been only kind and helpful, but Harold has lost his trust in me. I pray it's only the fever making him see things this way.

That part of the journal seems especially sad to me. That entry was the first one that hinted at why my great-great-grandparents separated. I stared at the farmhouse and imagined the one-room cabin that could very well be the central room in the old house.

After the snake bite, Mr. Brighton had taken in my grandparents and nursed both of them as best he could. He was a widower with a small son making a life here raising cows, sheep, and horses. My great-great-grandmother credited him with saving both their lives. Great-great-grandma feared for her pregnancy and her husband's leg. In Brighton's house she could rest, and he and my great-great-grandfather cared for her until great-great-grandpa's wound healed and the baby seemed okay. The two-week delay caused by their recuperating started the downhill slide for their marriage.

I drove over the City of Rocks Reserve boundary noticing the grass and sage looked verdant in the rain. It had been a wet winter with lots of snow, so things were still very green. I tried to imagine what the terrain would look like all dried out in high summer. The sagebrush would be the same green, but the grass would be much taller and yellow. Great-great-grandma had written that they'd set off from Salt Lake City on Pioneer Day; that's July 24th.

They would have had sufficient time to get to Sacramento safely, meaning they could clear the Sierra Nevadas before winter. Great-great-grandpa had been in the Mormon Battalion and had known the men who'd first found gold in northern California. However, he had chosen not to be a miner-forty-niner and had returned to Utah to rejoin his young wife and three small children.

He and that wife had grown apart, but instead of divorcing, he'd taken a second wife, my great-great-grandmother, following the then-Mormon practice of polygamy. My mom always said he'd not been following the prophet so much as following his pants with that decision. Regardless, tensions were high and it became clear that wife number one was not happy having her long-absent husband back and living next door with wife number two. I know many of the Mormon pioneers practiced plural marriage, and it helped populate the west, but I don't understand how any of the affected people were happy with polygamy. My curiosity about it motivated Mom to let me keep great-great-grandma's journal.

Reading her journal showed me great-great-grandmother was like any other young bride. She mentioned her husband's first wife and hinted that there was little love between the two wives, but she enjoyed helping raise the three kids and was looking forward to adding to the brood. And, each wife had her own house, so my great-great-grandmother experienced many of the things that other newlyweds did. Only in her case, her husband came to hate visiting his other wife and was determined to start over with great-great-grandmother in California. It was 1851, he was excited to move, and his cooper business would suit them well in either place. Everyone needed barrels, especially miners trekking into the mountains and needing supplies.

I approached the first large rocks in the park. I was looking for Camp Rock, where my great-great-grandmother had camped for the last time in the City of Rocks. Even in the rain, the granite formations were amazing. From a distance, their eroded forms looked like a cluster of huts or cottages, but up close their size amazes. Most are bigger than a house or a smaller multi-storied building. All are remnants of granite left after everything else had eroded away. And most are fun to walk on and climb. Camp Rock looks like a huge loaf of bread. I parked my Jeep nearby and checked the sky. The rain had stopped. The clouds were lightening in color, but still gray, and no sun poked through.

I walked the few yards needed to get close to the rock. The scale of City of Rocks makes the granite formations seem much smaller than they are until you're next to or on top of them. Camp Rock sat on a relatively flat granite field and made an excellent windbreak. Up close, I could see where the lee of the massive boulder had kept a dry spot. I imagined wagons parked here with livestock grazing nearby while fires were stoked in the shelter of the rock. Consulting my map showed where the pioneer names were found. Pioneers had graffitied their names and dates on the rocks by carving or using axel grease. I soon found the "T.L." I was looking for. Family lore hinted that it could have been made by Therese Linnet, my great-great-grandmother. The "T.L." was small and faded, but still discernible. It was just lower than my shoulders. I closed my eyes and imagined my great-great-grandparents camping here.

I pictured my great-great-grandmother cooking biscuits on the fire while great-great-grandpa settled the mules for the night. She was heavily pregnant but still mobile. They hoped to make it to Placerville a month before the baby was due.

I moved back toward the road and looked around. A small outcrop stood nearby. It sloped gently to rise about twenty feet up from the granite bedrock and looked like an overturned bowl. I walked to its summit and surveyed the scenery. I think this is how my great-great-grandmother found the courage to do what she did: standing on a high rock. Being up that high made my Jeep below look tiny. It empowered me; I'm sure it gave her a different perspective too. I recalled the next journal entry from Camp Rock that seemed to follow a fight between my great-great-grandparents.

Harold has asked me to decide and give him an answer in the morning. I remain unsure that what I must do is what I should do. As I behold this beautiful valley full of majestic granite carved into fantastical shapes seemingly by God's hands, I celebrate this beauty while Harold sees only the rocks standing in our way and laments the time lost. I think of our child, my first born. I believe he will be a boy, my husband's first son, and I weep in my heart for him. His father has turned against me. I've done nothing wrong, yet Harold says he has much to forgive. Agony fills me, but I feel that I must return to Utah. I cannot raise my son with a man who despises his mother. Nor can I ignore the wanderlust that forever rides my husband. I know now that he'll always yearn to move on, to gain more, and will never be satisfied. I wonder whether it would have been better for me to have acted improperly with Mr. Brighton. Surely those are a man and child who needed me. I confess I saw how the father looked upon me. Not lust, but coveting and envy for what my husband had. I gave him no cause to seek for what he wanted from me. But Harold saw his hunger and became convinced that though I did not invite his interest, I returned it. How I long for the trust of my husband. His first wife warned me, but I was blind. We both are victims of some other woman's perfidy. I wonder who she was to make our husband so unable to trust a woman. These words wander as do my thoughts. But I've found peace at last. I will return home. Harold's wives will raise his children in Utah.

On their last night together, my great-great-grandparents had camped here for another night. I don't know how well they slept or whether their final parting had been quiet or loud. The family stories say that Therese Linnet had spent a long while carving her initials in the tough old granite and then used a burnt stick from the

fire to blacken the marks. She'd marked the rock to show the
farthest point north she'd reached or would ever reach. She'd also
taken back her name. Linnet was her father's surname, not
Harold's.

A soft breeze pushed at me as I stood high. I saw blue sky finally
peeking through the clouds. The rain was moving out of the City of
Rocks. I closed my eyes and breathed deep, filling my lungs with the
fresh, moist air. I looked down at my feet and saw the sky reflected
in the water stored in tiny panholes in the rock. A feeling of warmth
and peace overtook me. I felt it tingle from the top of my head
through my body and out the ends of my fingers and toes. I learned
Therese was happier leaving the City of Rocks than entering it. I
headed down to Camp Rock. Mom wanted pictures of the rock and
its carving. She also wanted pictures of all the nearby houses and
homesteads. One of them used to belong to a Brighton family.

When I finished taking pictures I drove through and explored
the park some more. Some rocks need to be climbed to be experi-
enced and I loved scrambling on them. When I'd tired myself out
and the crowds got to me, I left the park the way I'd come. I'll come
back one day and either try the old road that leads to Kelton, Utah,
or head out the west entrance and come home via Burley, Idaho.

I smile as I think about how great-great-grandma finished her
aborted journey to California. This journal stops at Camp Rock,
but later ones and family records tell what happened next.

Therese did leave Harold at the City of Rocks. Actually he took
her back to Mr. Brighton where he left her, the wagon, and part of
their supplies. He immediately left for California with the two
mules, his cooper equipment, and his share of the supplies. From all
accounts he made good time and completed his journey well before
the snow flew. Sometime later he married for a third time and
started a new branch of the family that still populates northern
California today.

I don't know how Therese and Mr. Brighton agreed on it, but
instead of him selling her two horses for her wagon and maybe
escorting her to Salt Lake City, Mr. Brighton married Therese. She
had a little boy who was adored by his older stepbrother. Unlike

Harold, Therese divorced her first spouse, and she wasted little time marrying her second. Their first child together, a girl, was born to a Mr. and Mrs. Brighton within eleven months of her separation from Harold.

Therese doesn't write about how she and Mr. Brighton fell in love. Her later journals express the love that I imagine they enjoyed. Maybe Harold was right about his wife's inclination towards Mr. Brighton and she hadn't yet realized it. In the family, we joke that they must have loved each other very much. They had thirteen children together and both lived to see age 80.

As I drove home, I kept meditating on my great-great-grandmother's life and had just thought, "I hope that if I am ever in a situation like my great-great-grandmother's I will have the courage to turn back on a journey in order to find happiness," when my cellphone rang.

I recognized the number and felt my temper flare. I pulled to the side of the road and stopped. I killed the engine, because I figured talking to Liam could take some time. After six rings, the ringing stopped. If Liam stayed true to form, when he was upset, he'd call twice before leaving a message. He would then either wait five minutes before calling me again or send a flurry of text messages.

As he called the second time, I debated answering. I had an idea why he was calling. Because of our fight, to get some time and space to think about him, I'd taken this journey to City of Rocks.

The second ringing ended. The voicemail icon didn't appear, but texts did. Liam sent a short message in two texts: "Hannah, please call me. I need to talk to you." It made me sigh. I closed my eyes to think.

I recalled our fight and the things that led up to it. A tear dropped to my cheek. Liam and I had broke up after six months of steady dating. He'd hurt me deeply. The fight had started when I got fed up with him ignoring me. I'd finally noticed he'd been talking about himself without letting me speak, again. Mid-sentence, I interrupted him to say, "Oh, shut up. I'm tired of hearing about your job or your mom." Yes, I'd started the fight, but apparently I'd hit a nerve, because he'd responded with, "Well, that's better than talking about your stupid plans to open a bakery."

Those were such stupid things to say to each other. But, they started an argument that escalated. Now three days later, he wanted to talk. I thought about great-great-grandma and how my great-great-grandfather had shut her out. Was I being unreasonable? How much was I like Harold? Wasn't I more like Therese?

At that moment the clouds broke overhead, letting sunshine flood me in my Jeep. It felt like a sign, an omen. I didn't want to talk to Liam but felt that to be like Therese, I should talk to him at least one more time. Half-heartedly, I pushed the call button.

Of course he answered immediately. "Hannah? Where are you?"

"That's not important. What do you want to say to me?"

"I'd like to apologize, in person."

"That's not possible, Liam, I'm out of town."

"I know. Your mom told me. I'm near the City of Rocks. Where are you?"

My mind raced. I wondered how Liam had beat me here. I'd lost time running out of gas, but could he have driven past my Jeep and not stopped? Did he arrive while I was in the park?

"Hannah? Did you hear me? Look, I'm at the gas station in downtown Malta. Where are *you*?"

However we missed each other, he was here. I answered, "I'm about five minutes away. I'll meet you there."

"Good. Hannah..."

"Not now, Liam. We'll talk when I get there." I hung up on him.

I pulled in and parked next to Liam's Audi. He was leaning against the trunk watching me. I couldn't help noticing how good he looked. Our chemistry was never an issue. He came over to open my door. Like his tall, lanky looks and curly hair, his nice manners were not a problem for "us."

He stepped back slightly as I got out and said, "Thank you for meeting me, Hannah." He took my hands in his. "I'm sorry. I was wrong. I've been thinking about what you said, and you're right. I have been hogging our conversations and ignoring your input. Can you forgive me?"

He looked so hopeful and repentant. I looked away from him for a minute. I thought about his words and the fact that he'd driven so far to see me. Then I realized grand gestures would never fix our problems. However, I cared about him enough to give him a chance. I turned back to him. "Thank you, Liam. I appreciate your apology. I'm sorry that I lost my temper. The fight went too far."

He moved to embrace me. I held him off by lifting one hand. "Look, I'll give you another chance, but I've decided that while both of us need to better watch our words, I think I need to see some positive *actions*. So, let's plan on a 'reset,' starting with a date tonight."

"I can do that. But, what about now. I mean, how will your Jeep get home?"

I sighed. "Liam, that's why we need a reset. You make too many unilateral decisions for us. I'm not riding home with you. I'll drive my Jeep to my house and you'll drive your Audi to your house, and we'll meet for dinner later. I'll call you when I get home. I hope you'll use the drive to think some more. See you later."

"But..." he tried to stop me from leaving.

I brushed his arms away. "No, not now. It's time that I get a say in our relationship. I've let you have your way too much. I'm saying 'not now, but later.'" I stared in his eyes, and watched him fidget in my peripheral vision as he considered my words.

Finally, he met my look. "Okay. Drive safe."

"Thank you. I'll call you in a few hours."

I tried to stay calm as I backed my Jeep away. As I entered the highway, I looked at him in my review mirror. He was still standing where I'd left him outside his car. I couldn't stop a few tears, but I kept going. I would call him when I got home. It was time I took better care of my life. I passed a sign for the City of Rocks park and said a little prayer in honor of my great-great-grandmother. "Please, Lord, help me do the right thing so I can be happy like Therese became."

TWENTY

WAR ON WOAD

Matthew Funk

On a recent spring morning I was driving to work, watching the sun come up over the Rockies and the mountain valley that stretched green and fresh before me. In a few weeks, the heat and the summer would start turning most of the green to brown and farmers would start to water their crops, but at that moment all that was all in the future and the spring morning was the very essence of new life and possibility.

But then as I drove past a field of alfalfa, the peace of that spring moment was broken. I saw something sitting there in plain sight, as if watching me.

A hillside covered with a noxious weed known as Dyer's woad.

The morning breeze caressed the yellow flowers in a parody of comity and peace. A couple of thousand people drove past it that morning, but only I and perhaps a handful of others saw the plant for what it truly was.

Suddenly, it was a morning forty years or more gone—it was the late 1970s, and I was riding shotgun while my dad drove us in to town to get parts for one of the tractors.

It was quiet in the cab of the truck—just the sounds of the

engine and the road. Dad didn't say much while he was driving. His mind was usually elsewhere. He didn't care to be disturbed by questions he considered unimportant or trivial. I knew that if I had a serious question he'd be happy to answer it. Dad never concerned himself with existential questions about the intangibles of life. Those questions got short shrift. However, serious questions, like why alfalfa needed to be irrigated so often or why one wheat field had a more bluish color than another—those questions he was pleased to answer.

Certain other things could be counted on to draw my father's attention and entice him to break the quiet. Foremost among these was a good-looking field of corn. Dad admired a well-planted cornfield; it spoke not only to the skill of the planter, but also to good timing and favorable weather—a trifecta of craft, circumstance, and grace.

Dad taught me that a late frost stunted corn while a wet spring kept a farmer off the ground until the cool, more favorable temperatures had passed which forced the young corn to start later, when it was hotter. A good field of corn had to be planted at the right seed depth, with the right soil moisture, and during the infrequent breaks of cool, dry weather, after the risk of frost but before those precious mid-spring days were lost. Only the most favorable combination of moisture and temperature brought rapid growth to the blade and ear.

I remember my dad bestowing his stamp of approval on a corn field only a few times in my youth, most memorably on a field near Preston, Idaho, during the Reagan era.

"That's a good-looking crop of corn," he said.

What struck me about that moment was the respect in my father's voice. It was the tone of voice he might use when speaking to the father of the high-school quarterback who just won the state championship—"That's a fine young man you've got there."

Among farmers, fields were then—and still are—what in the business world we might call a "metric," a measure of a man's skill, savvy, and luck. Every summer, each crop was out there for all to see, each a testament of that farmer's ability to provide for his family and a statement about who was the best. Most people drove past the fields unaware of the subtext—town folk who probably couldn't identify what the crop was if you held a gun to their head. But to farmers, each field was like a billboard displaying your expertise and ability, readable in a heartbeat to others of the brotherhood.

Boys competed on the football field or in the Pinewood Derby. Their fathers competed more subtly but in far greater earnest. The men who were good at farming made their living on the land; those that were bad at it supplemented their income by driving a school bus or pushing a mop at the university. There was nothing wrong with that: they weren't bad men, they just weren't good farmers.

It was the later class of these men that drew my father's attention that late May morning during the Carter years.

"Matthew, look out there in Smith's field," said Dad.

I looked in the direction he'd indicated.

"Hell," he added, "A.J. has Dyer's woad right out there in the middle of that good-looking stand of alfalfa."

Dad's normally friendly voice dripped with rebuke. My father never thought much of this particular farmer and here was public proof of the man's weakness. Then and there I knew that A.J. Smith had done something low and wrong. I just didn't know exactly *what.*

I later learned that *Isatis tinctoria*, commonly known as Dyer's woad, is an invasive plant species that grows during the spring from a tall central stalk with small bright yellow flowers. Dyer's woad killed our hay, was unpalatable to the delicate palates of our Holstein cows and was a scourge that we couldn't seem to stop. Dad had spotted it right in the middle of A.J. Smith's field of hay as if the damn thing had personally picked the spot. Dad seemed to imply the woad was mocking us.

"You see what I mean," Dad said, still pointing. "You see it out there?" It was as though A.J.'s shame could not have been greater had his daughter gotten pregnant out of wedlock.

Anxiety shot into my heart. I was nine. At the time I didn't know what Dyer's woad looked like. I also suffered from an undiagnosed case of severe myopia, and couldn't see the woad even if I could have properly identified it. However, I knew that admitting my ignorance would mark me as something less than I should be, and more, it would be a sign of failure on my father's part: raising a son who even at age nine could not identify Dyer's woad. And if my father discovered that one of his sons couldn't spot Dyer's woad chances were that he'd pull over right there on the side of the road and cast me out of the family.

"Matthew," he'd have said in his stentorian voice ripe with judgment, "get out of the truck, and don't even bother to come home."

I had to make sure he never found out my taxonomic shortcomings.

"Yeah," I stammered. "I think I see it. I mean, yeah, it's right there?"

"*You think* you see it?" he grumbled suspiciously. "Hell, it's right out your window." He motioned dismissively toward the middle of the forty-acre hay field. It was a quarter-mile away if it was a yard.

Desperate to change the subject I asked, "Where does Dyer's woad come from?"

Ah, his son was asking a serious and important question. This would be an excellent opportunity to teach me the history and lore of Dyer's woad. There would be a quiz later.

"Well, Matt, Dyer's woad comes from Russia."

This sounded right given our current state of diplomatic affairs with the Soviets.

"It was brought to Utah by the pioneers to make dye for their clothes," Dad continued. "They grew it over in Box Elder County. But then they figured out it had no natural predators here and by then it was too late. It's been out of control ever since. Over in Box Elder it's all over the place. It's migrating its way down the Wasatch Front and into the canyons."

Dyer's woad apparently had a plan for world domination.

My father grew up during the Great Depression. He endured difficult times and saw a lot of poverty and tragedy. Dad's uncle Cyril and aunt Hazel and their five kids lived in a chicken coop for a while after the bank foreclosed on their house. I've been in that chicken coop; one big room, cement floor, watering trough, steeply sloped roof. On one side of the coop you could stand straight with plenty of head room. On the other side you couldn't. Dad's father, my Grandpa Leroy, was a county agricultural agent during the Great Depression, and at the time the family lived not far from an Indian reservation. Sometimes—when Grandpa was away—Indians would show up at the house and threaten Grandma until she gave them something to eat.

As far as my father was concerned, things were bad and always getting worse, and the rise of Dyer's woad was just more proof of that.

Sure, we'd won World War II, and we had graves of young men up in the town cemetery to prove it, but now the Japanese were selling us cheap cars and Detroit couldn't compete. The Commies were winning the Cold War and the world was going to hell. Closer to home, Paul Volcker was running the Fed and was aggressively raising interest rates to combat inflation. Gas was up to sixty-five cents a gallon, wheat was down to three dollars a bushel and it turned out that Rock Hudson was gay. The Cold War, the economic war, the oil embargo, and of course the seasonal wars farmers fought against the elements—everything was a war and nothing embodied that ethos like Dyer's woad.

Woad was the enemy, a plant that despite all efforts was spreading uncontrollably throughout the West. Left on its own, woad established itself in thick, monotypic stands that crowded out native plant species. Woad contributed to soil erosion, degraded live-stock forage and, as if that weren't enough, my father suspected woad infestations of weakening our community's moral strength.

As a boy growing up on his grandpa's farm, Dad had spent many hours pulling Dyer's woad by hand. Woad is incredibly resis-tant to herbicides, and the only really effective way to combat woad was pulling it by hand and disposing of the plant in mid- or late-May, before the seed pods released their payload. So, not only was it a war, it was hand-to-hand combat. Dyer's woad was really the perfect enemy for farmers to hate. My generation had to look for enemies—there were few real ones, so we searched our imaginations and came up with the Terminator and Darth Vader. My father's generation, well, their enemies were more existential. If you had a bad year and the crops failed or the cows got sick then you were raising your kids in a chicken coop on a concrete floor. Dyer's woad, with its bright, pretty yellow flowers and its alien ways seemed to smile at us as we drove by, a quiet menace and a silent promise.

Years after that May morning in the Carter era, I married a beautiful girl from Smithfield, a neighboring town. Her father, Ralph, was a dry-farmer and had four hundred acres out west past Trenton. Because of the rolling hills in the area, that part of the county was known as "the washboards". Ralph was a kind man, gentle in appearance and action; a man who cared deeply for his family. But it turned out that there was more to my father-in-law than the kind, middle-aged appearance he projected. He was a man with his own war to fight.

If Dyer's woad was a threat in Richmond, near our farm, it was an out-of-control infestation in Trenton. Trenton was much closer to the epicenter of the Northern Utah woad infestation in Box Elder County, and woad blanketed the Trenton hills like a yellow haze, a wildland of yellow blossoms advancing inexorably on all points of the compass. And more than that, the woad seemed to be a statement of Trenton's moral decay. A drive through the desiccated remains of downtown Trenton only served as confirmation of love's labor lost. The general store was a padlocked memory, and the farmers' cooperative was hanging on by its fingernails—it finally went down for the count a few years later.

In the face of such stark circumstances, Ralph Holt undertook his duty with quiet (but desperate) dignity. Ralph had two big advantages; he was determined and prolific. Ralph and Gloria Holt had six children, and twenty-six grandchildren and growing numbers of great-grandchildren. And every Memorial Day weekend Ralph would summon his progeny to battle against the woad. For decades, every three-day Memorial weekend, the clan would marshal and spend Saturday and Monday pulling and bagging Dyer's Woad on Ralph's four-hundred-acre farm. The intervening Sunday was reserved for holy worship at the town church and traveling to various local cemeteries to place chrysanthemums on the graves of ancestors.

There were no Memorial Day trips, no camping, no swimming. Just pulling Dyer's woad and visiting cemeteries. At times the grandchildren weren't sure which was worse, the woad pulling or the interminable trips to some dead relative's grave.

Then, after seven decades of sweat and sunburn, victory.

Ralph had done it. The family farm was free of the invader. The tens of thousands of acres around Trenton were still overrun with Dyer's woad, but Ralph Holt's four hundred acres was clear of the stuff. It was a sublime moment and the family labor force knew it and cheered. America had Victory-in-Europe day and Victory-in-Japan day, and the Holts had Victory-in-Trenton day. From then on, a few hours each spring would suffice to keep rogue woad from re-establishing a foothold on Ralph's family farm. Not many years later, his enemy vanquished, my father-in-law went to his eternal reward. Before he died, his sons having become engineers and accountants, he sold the farm.

My father has also gone to his eternal rest, and like Ralph, none of Dad's children are farmers, and so our farm suffered the same fate and was sold, piece by piece, field by field, until all that remains is the small fifty acre homestead my great-grandparents settled. It is mine now, as are the fruits and burdens of ownership. The war against Dyer's woad continues, but there are few who even know about it, and fewer still who fight it. The slopes of the Rockies are now tinged in yellow and the hills overlooking Richmond are becoming overrun with yellow monotypic stands of *Isatis tinctoria*. There are few family farms left in Cache Valley and those that are still here face a grim future; the war against Dyer's woad wasn't the only war lost.

I still farm the homestead, but I make my living as an accountant; my brothers work in other professional fields. This was by design. Dad could see no future in farming and made sure that his sons found other careers. As an adult, I've cried twice. The day my father died and the day we sold the cows. I'm the last, a fourth-generation farmer. There won't be a fifth.

At the end of every day I drive home from the office and watch the growing stands of woad spread year after year. But there are bright spots; in the truck with me are my four daughters. They've spent every Memorial Day of their childhood in Trenton and in Richmond pulling Dyer's woad, and they can spot the stuff at a half mile or more. And they know what to do with it.

TWENTY-ONE

CENTER OF THE SIEGE

Christine McDonough

After.

We wait.

Men with strange speech hold siege to our towers.
I pace snowy battlements behind archers and army
dredging my depths to staunch a bleeding hope
as my gown drags on flagstones laid by my blood.

In darkened rooms, blades of daylight invade through stone cracks
followed by devils and doubt slipping in with night air.
Those following a holy way sing matins and evensong,
whilst heathens whisper to a God long denied.

Staircases spiraling, echoing only footfalls and whistling wind.
From the Great Hall's arrogant oak rafters hang dense tapestries,
embroidery proclaiming fabled history of our wars and victories,
now shaming wounded soldiers lying below its lowest fringe.

We eat little and sleep less, carrying fatigue in bundles that warp our
spines.
Knees weaken, though spirits hold. *Our soldiers are coming,* I say.
But I lie. Two falcons released now, carrying our despair, neither
returned.
My inked feather scratches one last parchment to send by wing.

These words are brief and vital – though I send no secrets,
no counts of soldiers, patterns of patrol, points of weakness.
No, my spies have since died or fled or turned.

I pen careful words for my love, for when he brings the soldiers.
If we do not last, if we do not last, if we do not last.
The stars will shine. After.

Moon and sun will not even pause their chase.
But he will have my words to grasp. After.

If my center cannot hold this circle. If we do not last.

After.

We wait.

TWENTY-TWO

LOBSTER BISQUE

Chris Todd Miller

Portland Harbor, Casco Bay
Marion R Jensen Correctional facility
Rec Room

Free time in the rec-room at the Marion R Jensen Correctional facility in Portland, Maine resembled a playground, except there were no females, plenty of profanity, and in place of kickball, an old television clung to the wall. The corner of the screen was cracked, but the picture was clear. They even had a playground monitor, Correctional Officer Mendoza. A dozen inmates gathered around the idiot box.

Currently the Caucasians had the room, which today included a handful of skinheads. Access to the TV room rotated on a schedule between the Hispanics, Asians, Blacks, and the White Supremacists. Subcategories of those groups included everyone else: the mentally ill, the born-agains, the guys just trying to do their time, and any other hard ass that nobody wanted to mess with. As hard asses go, former Master Chief Petty Officer Curtis Oliver of the US Navy Seals was the baddest motherfucker on the block.

A dispute started over what to watch. Before things got heated they realized the channel was stuck on a local affiliate showing a *Friends* rerun. "Who the fuck was watching this?" asked Warchild, the skinhead leader.

"Probably a schitzo," replied another follicle-challenged brother.

Curtis smirked. *It was rhetorical, you dumb hick.*

Warchild left, taking most of his cronies with him. Everyone else settled down to watch *Friends*, given it was their only option.

A new face pulled an orange plastic chair near Curtis and sat down. "Oh, this is the one where Phoebe tells Ross that Rachel is his lobster and she's his."

"Spoiler alert," Curtis glared at the new guy. "Look, I don't know who you are but I have two questions: one, what're you talking about? And two: who the hell are you and why are you sitting next to me?"

"That was three questions."

"You have exactly three seconds to get the fuck out of my face," Curtis said.

The man put up his hands in a surrender gesture. "I'm Petty Officer 3rd Class, James Coleman, sir. You are Curtis Oliver and you're a goddamn legend."

Curtis looked at James for a long second. "That was a good answer. You can stay, for the moment."

James slid his chair closer. His face shone like he was just asked to prom by the head cheerleader.

"You know my story?"

"Yes sir," said James. "I don't blame you one bit, either. That son-of-bitch had it coming. He got off easy if you ask me."

"Oh, I see. So you actually don't know shit."

"Sir?"

"Just answer my other question," Curtis said pointing at the television.

"Oh, yes sir."

"And stop calling me sir. That's not who I am anymore."

"Yes si—um, okay. This is the episode where Ross is freaking out because he thinks he might lose Rachel and to calm him down

Phoebe explains how lobsters mate for life and Ross and Rachel are lobsters to each other."

"And this was a hit show?" Curtis asked. "It's bullshit, by the way."

"The show?"

"Yeah, but the lobsters, too. That's not how they mate. Lobsters get it on with several mates."

James scrunched his face. "Really, how do you know that?"

Curtis leaned forward and put his forearms on his knees. "Like I said, you don't know shit about me. If you did, you'd know that before I ended up in here, my wife and I ran a lobster trawler. She still does, in fact."

"You were the captain of a troller?"

Curtis shook his head. "Trawler." He emphasized the AW. "And I never said I was the captain. That's my woman. We own it, but I do whatever she says from emptying traps to eatin' pussy."

James nodded his head in deep contemplation. Curtis slapped James's knee with the back of his hand. "You got a lady waiting on you?"

"Yeah, yeah I do."

"Then you'd be wise to follow my advice. What's her name?"

"Freyja. And she's pregnant. Due in a few months."

"No shit. When do you get out?"

"A lot longer than a trimester. This new administration is going to deport her and there's not thing one I can do about it."

"You married?"

"Engaged. Even if we were married, Trump's ban would still kick her out."

"Hashtag MAGA," Curtis spat.

Portland Harbor, Casco Bay
Marion R Jensen Correctional facility
The Prison Yard

Curtis and James met regularly in the yard. Curtis shared war stories and James, who never saw combat, shared Icelandic culture. James was convicted of forgery and immigration fraud trying to loophole the citizenship process for his fiancée. They met while James was stationed at the US Naval Base in Iceland at the Keflavik International Airport. When Curtis prodded him for details, all James would say was, "it's complicated."

On this day, the wind blew off the harbor and carried to the prison yard with a unique crispness. "It's its own kind of punishment, you know?" Curtis said. "Putting us this close to the ocean and making it so far away." They watched the trawlers come and go around the oil tankers, ferries, cargo and cruise ships, and the handful of yachts.

"Did you see that?" Curtis asked.

"What?"

"See those trawlers to the north. Look for a flashing light. That's my Jessie. She flashes that halogen light three times to let me know she's close."

"That's the most romantic thing I've ever heard," said James. They stared at the harbor for a minute or maybe an eternity; Curtis wasn't sure.

"Let's think about something else," James said. "What's the first thing you're going to eat when you get out?"

"That's easy, lobster bisque. Jessie makes the best lobster bisque in New England."

They walked alongside the chain link fence, razor wire circled the top. James picked up a rock and threw it over. "You've never told me her name before."

"Yeah, well, I'm starting to not not like you."

"Sea captain and she can cook. Doesn't get much better than that."

"No, it doesn't," Curtis smiled and winked. They walked for a few more minutes.

"Can I ask you something else?"

"You can ask," replied Curtis.

"What's your real story? You said I don't know shit about you. What don't I know?"

Curtis squatted on his heels and sighed. "I never killed anyone. I mean, outside of a sanctioned maneuver. I know everyone here tells you they're innocent, but I really am." He stood and they continued to pace the perimeter. "Jessie's dad died right after she was born. When she was sixteen, her mother remarried. Before long, her step-dad started touching her and it escalated from there. When she turned eighteen, she left. Got work as a deckhand. Worked her way up to first mate. Eventually, we met, bought a boat, and went into business for ourselves."

"You walked away from the SEALS to catch lobster?"

"I was in a dark place, Jimmy." He looked out over the bay. "She silenced the demons. I think it's because she'd beaten her own demons. There's not much that salt water can't cure."

"What did you name your boat?"

"Blank Check. It was the key to our earning potential, a veritable boatload." He laughed at his own joke. "It also symbolized what we were trying to do. A clean slate. A fresh start."

"But then?"

"Step-dad knocked up Jessie's mom. Ultrasound said girl. Jessie about lost it. There's no way on God's green Earth she would let what happened to her happen to her sister. She found her step-dad and shot him. There's no way in hell I'd let my woman go to prison. I took the fall. I had a good lawyer. Got it knocked down to manslaughter. Now I'm here, and she's out there."

"I can't imagine doing that. I mean, I'd want to, I just don't know that I could."

"You could. For the woman who quiets the demons, you could do anything."

They stopped near a corner of the yard. "You see this spot?"

"Here where we're standing?"

"Yeah. Remember it."

"Why?"

"It's a dead spot. Come on, let's head back. Hey, are you any good at forgery? I mean you're here so maybe you suck at it."

"I'm good. I'm real good. Like I said, it's complicated."

As they approached the main area, Warchild stepped in front of Jimmy. "Where have you two lovebirds been?"

Curtis motioned Jimmy behind him. "Leave it alone, Warchild."

"Leave what alone? Your boyfriend? I knew you two were fags. Come 'ere sweetheart, I'll show you a real man."

Warchild reached for Jimmy. Curtis grabbed Warchild by the wrist, did a step-pivot-twist and Warchild was on the ground. Curtis put a foot on his throat and didn't release the wrist hold. The skin-head circle moved in.

"Back the fuck off," Curtis said. He didn't yell it. He didn't need to. "Try something and he'll be jerking off lefty for the rest of his life." He applied more pressure to Warchild's wrist. "Do we understand each other?"

"Fuck you," Warchild said.

Curtis applied more pressure.

"Yes, goddammit," he said through clenched teeth. "Everybody, back off."

"Say you understand."

"I understand. God, please. I understand."

Curtis released him. He motioned to Jimmy and they walked away.

"I can handle myself," Jimmy said.

"I know you think you can."

James scoffed. "Then why?"

"Like I said, I'm not not liking you more and more, Jimmy."

———

The next morning Curtis and Jimmy sat across from each other at a table near the middle of the pod. Two trays sat between them consisting of oatmeal, eggs, toast, and sausage links.

Curtis cut up his sausage and mixed it with the oatmeal.

Jimmy speared a link and put it in his mouth.

"I wouldn't do that," Curtis said.

Jimmy made a face as if he'd just licked the floor. Curtis put a hand over his mouth. "Swallow it. If the guards see you spit it out that's all you'll get for a week."

Jimmy choked it down.

"The oatmeal makes it go down easier." He removed his hand. "About your special skills. Let's say I found a way out of this place."

"I'm listening."

"If I take you with me, can you make passports and other documents?"

"Absofuckinglutely, but I'm not going anywhere without my Freyja."

Curtis sporked a mouthful of eggs into his mouth. "Jessie will pick her up and meet us at a designated time and place, then we make a run to Canada."

"The dead spot?"

Curtis nodded. "The dead spot."

Portland Harbor, Casco Bay
   Marion R Jensen Correctional facility
   The Dead Spot

A handful of stars fought a losing battle with the pre-dawn. Curtis and Jimmy slipped away from the work detail where they were supposed to report to laundry. Officer Rodriguez would make sure their absence went unnoticed until it was too late. They followed the fence until they reached the dead spot where Jessie would be waiting with bolt cutters and his beloved SIG Sauer P226, just in case.

They made it through the yard without incident. When they reached the dead spot, Jessie wasn't there. Curtis scanned the area looking for her. "Jessie!" he whispered and yelled at the same time.

"Where is she?" Jimmy asked.

"She'll be here."

"We don't have—"

"There," Curtis pointed at dark figured, approaching north by north-east. "Come on, baby, daylight's coming."

There was no prescribed love scene like in the movies, they didn't kiss between the chain-link or grasp hands. Jessie just went to work with the bolt cutters.

"You're a minute late. What happened?"

"Ground patrol was late. Idiots. I nearly ambushed *them*. I'm surprised you haven't broken out of this place on your own by now." She worked the bolt cutter with an easy rhythm. She'd cut through about a dozen links when Curtis grabbed the fence with both hands and wrenched back the opening. Jimmy wriggled through then he held the opening for Curtis.

"Did you bring it?" Curtis asked.

Jessie gave him a WTF look and withdrew a Sig Sauer and shoulder holster from a nap sack.

"Come to me, baby."

Jessie handed it to him and he cinched it up with a practiced movement. Jessie already wore hers.

"You both have one?" Jimmy asked.

"Jessie, this is Jimmy."

Jessie cocked her head. "Where'd you find this guy?"

Curtis laughed. "Iceland, as it turns out."

She looked at Jimmy. "Freyja's on my trawler. She's fine but we need to go." She looked at Curtis. "And for you, a thermos of lobster bisque waits below deck."

"Can't wait."

"Does that mean what I think it means?" Jimmy asked.

Alarms shattered the peaceful morning. Spotlights raced each other across the yard and stopped on the three fugitives.

"Shit, go," Curtis yelled. The three of them took off down the hillside, Jessie in the lead. The terrain was largely kept clear to deter escapees, but the city also had an ordinance that basically said it needed to look pretty. Clumps of trees dotted the area, partially obscuring the prison and still giving the locals their fall colors.

The three zig-zagged from clump to clump until they ran out of trees. Between them and the bay was a hundred yards of open ground. An ATV crested the rise to either side of them, their headlights blazed into the remnants of the night. Curtis put a hand on the back of Jimmy and Jessie, pushed them forward and yelled, "Go."

The three sprinted for the dock. Curtis calculated the intercept point. They weren't going to make it. He stopped and fired his Sig at one ATV then turned on the other. He aimed high, hoping the shots would slow them down. It worked. The pursuers came to a halt, only to pull out rifles and return fire.

Jessie and Jimmy stopped when they heard the shots.

Curtis went down.

Jimmy froze.

Jessie shrieked.

Jimmy did an awkward dance as he tried to flee and run back to Curtis at the same time. Jessie sprinted back to her Master Chief. "Come on," she yelled. When she reached him, she turned and laid down cover fire in one direction while Curtis mirrored her. Curtis yelled at Jimmy, "Go, get to the boat!" Jimmy bee-lined it for the dock, but hesitated before boarding.

Curtis fired a shot over his head and waved him on. Jimmy would have sense enough to know that meant shove-off and don't look back.

Jessie put his arm around her shoulder and the two of them humped it back to the nearest cluster of trees. Through the crimson and gold leaves, they watched their Blank Check merge into the harbor traffic and disappear.

She looked at his wound. "How much time do we have?"

"Two minutes, maybe less. Look, they don't know about you. I can get you a head start."

"Shut the fuck up."

He blinked back tears. "If you stay, know this: I'm not going back to prison."

She slapped a new magazine into her Sig, racked the slide, and kissed him. "I go where you go."

ABOUT THE AUTHORS

Virginia Babcock has always loved romantic fiction, and now writes her own stories of love and life in the real world. Virginia lives in northern Utah where she works full-time when she's not writing books. Her husband and cat keep her constantly entertained the rest of the time.

Elizabeth Watson Barnes grew up in Salt Lake City, Utah and now resides in Utah County. She's a nice person who laughs easily and is pathologically secretive about her private life. Writing fiction is the hardest thing she has ever done on purpose.

Robyn Buttars is an award-winning writer. Her work includes novels, stories for children, poetry, and music. She loves spending time with family and friends, traveling, and reading. Inspiration for a new creative project makes her day; being able to complete the project and share it with others is a special gift.

Denis Feehan writes primarily humorous short stories and poems, several of which have been published in print or on-line. He is the current president of the Heritage Writer's Guild in St. George, Utah. In addition to writing, Denis is the keyboard player for the Dealt-A-Straight band in Mesquite, NV. In his spare time, Denis is an actor and director at the Mesquite community Theater.

Matthew Funk is a fourth generation farmer and lives on the family farm in Northern Utah.

Brenda Birch Gallaher is a multi-award winning author who writes creative non-fiction and fiction. She is the middle child of five and has plenty of childhood memories to use for her creative non-fiction stories. She works as an administrative assistant at South-eastern Louisiana University at the same time she is earning her BA in English with a concentration in Creative Writing. Brenda hopes to continue to write and submit to the League's annual writing contest, and of course win. She is slowly but surely working on her novel.

Krystal Gerber is a student who still hasn't been kissed in the basketball student section, but she has a year or two before gradua-tion to make it happen. As vice-president of her university sketch comedy club, Krystal writes and performs humorous sketches ranging in subject from spies to Santa Clause. With the League of Utah Writers, Krystal has won first place in Romance and Flash Fiction, as well as second place for Speculative Fiction and Honor-able Mention for New Writer Fiction. Krystal has been published for two years in a row with LUW Press, while also creating funnily informative articles that are published across the web. To eat, Krystal is an assistant radio producer and writer for BYURadio. You can connect with Krystal on Facebook @authorKrystalGerber, on Twitter @krystalcgerber, or through email at krystalgerb@gmail.com.

Robin Glassey grew up in a small town with a leaky nuclear power plant, giving her the ability to randomly deactivate electronic devices. She graduated from BYU with a BS in Psychology and now analyzes her four boys, converts people to Doctor Who, and writes clean YA fantasy. In *The Azetha Series*, Robin transports readers to a world of sorcery and secrets. But although Robin writes about epic journeys, if she ever went on one, she'd die within the first mile.

Lorin Grace was born in Colorado and has been moving around the country ever since, living in eight states and several imaginary worlds. She graduated from Brigham Young University with a degree in Graphic Design. Currently, she lives in northern Utah with her husband, four children, and a dog who is insanely jealous of her laptop. When not writing Lorin enjoys creating graphics, visiting historical sites, museums, and reading. Lorin is an active member of the League of Utah Writers. Her debut novel, *Waking Lucy*, was awarded a 2017 Recommend Read award in the LUW Published book contest. *Mending Fences* received a 2018 Recommend Read award in the LUW Published book contest.

Amanda Hill's passion for writing is second only to her passion for reading. She recently won first place in the New Voices Fiction category with the League of Utah Writers. When she isn't writing or reading, she is knitting her way through closets of yarn, or supporting arts in the community by being costume director for plays, or serving on the South Jordan City Arts Council. She lives in South Jordan, Utah with her husband and five children.

Josie Hume is the author of several published short stories and articles including *The Cottage*, *Waiting for You*, and *Raising Kids*. Her love affair with writing started at an early age. Her first work was a Christmas play written on an old typewriter and performed by her siblings. Since then, she's enjoyed writing about her modern-day pioneer up-bringing, her year abroad, her adventures in the Marine Corps, and the continuing romance of a wonderful life. When she's not writing, she's building her house, playing with her five kids, traveling with her husband, or curled up with a good book. You can find her at josiehume.com.

Jef Huntsman is a lover of creativity, and no, his wife is not a jealous mistress. He taps out thrillers, memoirs, and poetry on his ever-failing laptop. He is the award- winning author of five novels including "Heart Attack, Yak, Yak," and his Carson thrillers, "Jamaica Rush" and "Mosquito Sands," published by Belray Books and a poetry book, "Bald Cats and Dead Elephants." His two newest books will be published in 2020.

Lorraine Jeffery has a bachelor’s degree in English, a MLIS in library science, and has managed public libraries in Texas, Ohio and Utah. She has won poetry prizes in state and national contests and published over sixty poems in journals and anthologies, including C*lockhouse, Kindred, Calliope, Ibbetson Street, Rockhurst Review, Orchard Press, Bacopa Press, League of Utah Writers,* and *Riverfeet.* Her short stories and essays have appeared in many publications, including *Persimmon Tree, Focus on the Family, Mature Years, Elsewhere* and *League of Utah Writers.* She has ten children (eight adopted) and lives in Utah with her husband.

C.H. Lindsay is a writer, award-winning poet, housewife, and mother, but not necessarily in that order. While she hasn't worked at a regular job since her kids were born, she spent thirty years as an event planner, organizing and running science fiction, fantasy, and horror conventions. She also spent a decade acting in musicals. Now she prefers to stay at home with her family, write novels, short stories, and poetry. She runs a fleet of online text-based roleplaying simulations. She has short stories and poems in ten anthologies, two more to be published in the next year. Her works have also appeared in several magazines, including "The Leading Edge," "Amazing Stories," and "Space and Time Magazine." She is working on two novels she hopes to complete in the next year or two. Mostly blind due to a degenerative eye disease, she collects print books for her library and audiobooks for herself. She is a member of SFWA, HWA, SFPA, and LUW. She is a founding member of the Utah Chapter of the Horror Writers Association. She lives in Utah with her "seeing-eye husband," youngest son, and two cats, who also consider themselves to be children.

Christine McDonough is an accomplished writer and poet. In 2019, she received an award for her short opera libretto, "The Stone, the Tree, and the Bird," from the Utah Opera opera competition, premiered May 2019. Her short story "Buried in the Witch raven's book" appears in *Oxford's Haunted,* an anthology of the Oxford Writing Circle 2018. Her education includes a MA in Information Design from the University of Reading (UK), as well as a Master of HR from Michigan State University. Christine is a home-grown Utahn, works as a writer and content developer at WGU Labs. She has achieved Photographer of the Year Bronze Level from the Professional Photographers of America and dabbles in archery, Irish drumming, and wheel-thrown pottery. She enjoys camping in Utah's Redrock country, but also loves to venture around the world.

Chris Todd Miller believes in the power of a well told story. He is a former president of the League of Utah Writers and a recipient of the League's Gold Quill Award for speculative fiction.

John Saporito was born and raised in lower New York. He has traveled the country in pursuit of fish, nature, and inspiration for writing. His work is saturated with a reverence for wild places and the creatures he uncovers on his nighttime visits to the sea.

Valarie Schenk is a creative based in Roy, Utah who serves through art and writing in order to assign meaning to personal experiences and communicate lessons learned through living. It is her deepest desire that these efforts promote and create safe spaces where people can connect with one another and heal alongside a friend.

Richard Timothy and the written word have not always gotten along. Growing up dyslexic, reading felt more like a punishment than something to enjoy. Sure, Superman had to deal with Lex Luther, but Richard had to deal with the weekly spelling bee in front of the entire class, and has yet to encounter a more profound evil. Despite this, he's always enjoyed writing stories. When the words didn't come out right, he kept at it until they did. As a result, he is now an award-winning writer and poet. To find out more about Richard and to see where he is currently published, check out his website: richardtimothy.com.

Marie Tollstrup was raised on a Wisconsin potato farm. At four-teen she joined the School Sisters of St. Francis in Milwaukee, WI, and taught as Sister Della, a nun, for ten years in Schiller Park and Wilmette, IL. Marie left the order at thirty-one and moved to CA where she eventually founded, advised, and produced *STYLUS*, a national award winning literary/art magazine at Jordan High School in north Long Beach for 23 years. After teaching full-time for 39 years, she retired in 1997 and launched her own writing career. Marie has won numerous awards for her writing at the national, state, and local levels. Her poetry has been published in *The Southern Quill, Panorama, Utah Sings*, seven LUW anthologies, and the *St. George Magazine*.

Johnny Worthen is an award-winning, best-selling, multiple-genre, tie-dye wearing author, voyager, and damn fine human being! Trained in stand-up comedy and modern literary criticism, Johnny is an instructor at the University of Utah, a professional author and editor.

Bryan Young is an award-winning author, filmmaker, and jour-nalist who works in many different media. As a writer, he's had numerous novels and short stories published and has worked profes-sionally in the Star Wars, Robotech, and BattleTech universes. His most recent novel is *BattleTech: Honor's Gauntlet*. He's written comics for Slave Labor Graphics and Image Comics and written and produced documentary films that were called "filmmaking gold" by the New York Times. As a journalist, he's had bylines at the Huffin-gton Post, StarWars.Com, HowStuffWorks, /Film, Syfy, and many more. He's the president of the Salt City Genre Writers, a Salt Lake City-based chapter of the League of Utah Writers, and also serves on the state board of that organization as Historian. He teaches writing for Writer's Digest and the University of Utah. You can learn more about him by following him on Twitter @swankmotron or by visiting his website, www.swankmotron.com.